I0532339

SPIRITUAL CONSCIOUSNESS NOW

BE HERE NOW - FOCUS ON AWAKENING - TRANSFORM YOUR LIFE - SEARCH ENLIGHTENMENT

Klaus Labuttis

BE PRESENT

ISBN 979-8-9888730-0-6

❀ Created with Vellum

Acclaim

Praise for Spiritual Consciousness Now

≈

"Klaus Labuttis has written a sensitive, discerning, and instructive record of his spiritual life. It is unpretentious, revealing clearly how he responds to the ongoing challenges of existence. Any person reading this book will find value in it. It is clear, it is to the point, and it is accessible."

Hugh James, author of "The Story of Man: A History of the Great Spiritual Tradition."

"Klaus Labuttis reveals in this book a sincere spiritual work. He shares his way of working with oneself to attain a higher level of existence which can teach us how to bring more consciousness to our own daily lives by using similar methods he shares in this book. This book can help those seeking a life with more profound meaning and fortify the conscious aspect of the Universe."

Tania Helft, author of "Spiritual Thoughts JOURNEY: Inspirational and motivational esoteric thoughts for every day of the year"

Foreword and Dedication

∼

This book results from 40 years of dedicating my life to finding the reason why I exist, searching for who I am, and developing the faculty in me that can love and Be Present.
This book is not the end of my journey but rather a milestone in expressing my Understanding of Awakening, its specific obstacles, and personal challenges.

Finally, the words have become a precise meaning, a guiding light into Being.

I dedicate this book to my Teacher, Robert Burton, who has opened the door of my prison. His love and focus on Being Present have guided me on the path of "Traveling Souls."

Preface

~

This book is a spiritual guidebook, an inspiration for anybody who understands that the Presence is all we have, a journey into Awakening.

All my life, I was fascinated with the stories of other people, the stories about adventurers and explorers traveling to the world's remote places.

Later in life, different adventures captivated my mind: the explorations of the Soul and my experiences with the Higher States of Consciousness.

At this time, I never imagined that Awakening and Spiritual Consciousness was my life's ultimate calling. Life's pleasures and external stimuli muted the voice I had not heard for a long time.

Today, I know that everything that has happened in my life was to prepare me for my appearance, for the transformation to Be.

When I truly realized that this Present Moment is all I ever have, I started to walk my path of Enlightenment. This realization was not simply knowledge but a deep feeling about my personal truth in life. Understanding this and deciding to make conscious efforts the primary focus within my life began the first step in my walk. Everything else was just preliminary preparations.

This book is my journey into Spiritual Consciousness, my travels into happiness and simplicity. My story is your story. Right now, you are looking for answers in your quest for transformation. I have given you mine.

Maybe they will help you to walk the "Road for Traveling Souls."

Klaus Labuttis, Oregon House, California

Bonus Book

~

The Sequence of Awakening - Ancient Conscious Teachings Revealed
Spiritual Exercises and Confirmation

Because you have taken an essential step towards your Enlightenment by purchasing this book, I'd like to give you a little gift.

The Ancient Technique for Awakening used by Conscious Schools throughout history

The Sequence of Awakening

is the core of my daily practices to Be Present.

It is a powerful method to

Grasping The Moment
Giving Up Identifications
Experiencing My Life in Harmony With Higher Forces

In addition, I have added some exercises I use in different life situations that help me stay present and not lose my precious Self. It is designed for those situations where we are most mechanical, like eating, driving, or using technical devices.

Get it Now!

Introduction

~

"Don't be satisfied with stories of how things have gone with others. Unfold your own Myth" Rumi

My old Mercedes Benz 240D was the only reliable aspect of my life when I drove to West-Berlin, Germany, in 1984. Fully packed with all my belongings and a willingness to explore a new life, I was otherwise lost and devastated. The woman of my dream, my soulmate, Esther, had abandoned me for another man, and I was filled with self-pity and tears. The pain was ripping me apart. I would sit aimlessly for hours in my room, unable to think about anything other than my misery. The only thing that could cure me of this love disease was to change my life completely.

No other place was more suitable than West Berlin. The former German capital, now divided in the middle of East Germany, was then full of opposites and strange realities.

I left Mannheim, the city I was born in, for the first time in 1981 to experience India and Nepal on a year-long journey. My hometown was a grey industrial area destroyed in the war to almost half what it used to be. Close to Heidelberg, the charming village of culture and philosophy, where, after common rumors, the American B52 bombers did not throw bombs but leaflets, indicating they would like to visit the city after the war.

After traveling through India and Nepal, my life changed dramatically. I finally moved away from my mother's house and joined a commune in a vast apartment on the grounds of the small airport in Mannheim. We had to share part of the property with the flight control tower there.

My friend Wolfgang, an experienced world traveler I met during a summer job in a margarine factory, organized the whole thing. Our incredible 10,000 square feet terrace was the hotspot for wild parties where dozens of friends and friendly strangers congregated. These gatherings became almost legendary in this midsize town of 300,000 inhabitants.

Not only did I have a change in scenery, but coming back from India also wholly altered my ideas and convictions, so continuing my studies at the University of Mannheim in Political Science and History was out of the question. This period opened a new, previously unknown world for me. It led me to study astrology, the books of Mystics and Philosophers, and especially the writings of two Russian Philosophers, George Gurdjieff and Peter Ouspensky, whose system of the 'Fourth Way' captured my attention.

Although my life had been a fantastic joyride in the last few years, full of wild, youthful, worry-free experiences, the

Russian Philosophers had initiated my journey to becoming a free spirit on my terms.

My spiritual search, at that time, was a timid exploration of all kinds of mind-altering experiences, including the daily consumption of Hashish and Marihuana.

But it was the beginning of a paradigm shift, and the drug-induced mental experiences led me more and more on a path where I questioned my old belief system. I realized another world was out there, but I had no idea how to grasp it and make it my own.

A road trip through East Germany during that time was a surreal experience. You could drive to West Berlin from West Germany through three major corridors. These transit zones had fortified checkpoints where the East German border and military guards treated you distinctly nasty.

Long-waiting periods were always the norm to get through all the paperwork and physical checks. I clearly remember the icy stare of one of the border guards as he checked my passport, sensing the hate and negativity oozing through his eyes. It created a conscious awareness in me, an understanding of how awful it must be for this man always carry this hate. I shuddered due to his cold glare and felt sadness for him. Some conscience had suddenly appeared in me, and I became aware of another human being in a different light.

One could not deviate from the official route and could only stop at specially guarded rest areas, where the so-called "Inter Shops" invited travelers to purchase cheap vodka and chocolate for their sought-after currency, the West Deutschmark.

These Kafkaesque experiences became common in my life while in West Berlin. I often went for a day to the other side, East Berlin, to see the museums, go to concerts and the Opera and buy some books with the mandatory exchange of twenty West Deutschmark for twenty East Deutschmark. Spending twenty East Mark in one day was challenging when everything was artificial and cheaply priced.

When I arrived in West-Berlin in 1984, lovesick and emotionally lost, I lived in one of these beautiful old apartments with high ceilings, stucco, large wood ovens, and huge rooms. The place was for sale, but I could stay there until the owner sold it.

I lived a monk's life in this magnificent place. I was without furniture besides a futon as a bed, a stool, and a table as kitchen equipment. I can still see my clothes hanging on nails from the walls in the bedroom as a form of art pieces instead of real art.

This humble place was the beginning of my journey and where my first Awakening took place, my coming into Being, the Waking up from my lifelong sleep of oblivion.

I vividly remember the evening in my empty flat in Berlin-Kreuzberg. For the first time, I felt alive. It was the end of October on one of these late autumn days when the wind was blowing hard, and everything and everybody was dancing in its path. I took my bike to one of my favorite places in Berlin, Charlottenburg Palace, a magnificent Baroque palace with beautiful Gardens filled with old

Chestnut-, Maple, and Oak Trees. The trees bowing to the force of nature and the sound of rustling leaves and aching branches wrapped me in a state of high alert.

Finally, exhausted but fully alert, I bicycled home and felt that this day's impressions had shifted something in me. I could not explain how or what, but I became restless and full of inner tension. My head felt hot, the point between my two eyes began to itch, and I started to see the things in my place more pronounced, more vivid, and more in focus.

Later that evening, I experienced my *Higher Self** for the first time in all its glory. I was God-like. I saw the world, which was full of justice and divine quality. I created a new human being, my *Higher Self**, and a clear light shined on my forehead. My eyes reflected this Moment in the rainbow of happiness. I prepared the table for opulence and richness; I designed the fruits of abundance and the wine to be drunk with the beauty of life.

I understood the richness of my life, the messenger of love asking me to abandon my fears and negativity. I was so resentful at this time, burdened with the weight of despair and suffering. My fear of living well had taken over the last few months, but suddenly a light was switched on, guiding me to my heart.

This bright light created love and compassion that filled me with joy, and a new understanding gave way: the knowledge of being alive, being here in this Moment. I accepted it humbly, asking forgiveness for my previous acts of hate and resentment. I understood my challenge in this life, and I received it. It was marvelous to be alive; it was beautiful to face my existence.

This Awakening lasted for several minutes as I sat in my empty flat. My Soul appeared; it was looking through my eyes. I was just the vessel in which it came alive. I do not know precisely how to explain such an experience - but these moments of Presence changed my life. I became a different man. I understood that my life has a meaning and a purpose, and there was no more time left to stay lingering in the unknown.

In the following years, I experienced Spiritual Consciousness in seeing the world and myself in all its beauty and harmony. The ability to be in the Moment gave me a taste of real life, a flavor I can never forget and will always desire.

Years before, I had reached similar states with the help of psychedelic drugs like LSD and magical mushrooms. But these experiences are shallow, a trick, a hoax, not comparable to the creation of oneself through effort and love.

That evening, I truly transformed my life. I had given up the drugs for the divine. I was in love with my *Higher Self*; why would I need any artificial substances to be Me?

These experiences started my fairytale of Awakening. Fairytales always need suffering and transformation. When you are in your darkest moments, you can begin to look up and experience the power of Awakening. That particular evening, I allowed myself to Be. Before, I felt like a misunderstood man with so much potential, and nobody saw it. But then my Soul appeared, and I saw my life as a guided journey to reach Presence.

I am Here Now; the fusion made me into the New Man. Because of my experience, I dedicate this book to my Awakening and your Awakening. Let us meet in the Garden of Love, where the flowers' fragrances never vanish. The beauty of our life is unfolding, and the fruits of our love for each other taste so sweet. Never allow anybody to question this miracle. Never let anyone tell you otherwise. We can't see anything other than miracles.

The reality of Awakening is not easy to bear. But what choice do we have when seeing the light shining and our inner Sun rising? Pain is the fire of love. Suffering is the heat that makes us tender.

It is painful to see the other self, unaware of the beauty of being in this Moment—the other part inside me whose expression is full of judgment, envy, and anger. I see the lies, the imagination that is the agenda of this other self. The *lower self**, ego, or false personality, the enemy within, wants to destroy our *Soul* and Presence.

Although I pray for my deliverance from these devilish forces, my efforts to replace them with love, forgiveness, and consideration sometimes fall short.

However, my gained awareness has allowed me to detect these attacks quickly. Before, I buffered these realizations with excuses and denial. I kept them hidden in the dark. Now I cannot close my eyes to my shortcomings or the empty words that often escape my tongue.

Instead of the fear of acknowledging the real me, there is now the perception of freedom, a sense of having to experience my humble human existence to move on. In doing so, I see my hand moving, the fingers obeying the thoughts to grasp a water glass. I see the dim light, the shadow of my body reflected onto the wall. I am here; I am present; I am happy and content.

Why was I afraid To Be Here Now? Why fear when it is all I have always wanted to be? Only in my moments of Presence do I truly possess Myself.

Although the pain remains, it does not frighten me anymore. Realizing that my life is full of contradiction is part of the journey.

I recall a Buddhist saying: *"When you reach the top, keep climbing."*

I keep climbing, embracing my *Higher Self**, although my reach is often weak. Sometimes I fear that my outstretched arm is more about pushing away the Gods than drawing them closer to me.

"This book is not a book. It touches you," as my guide, Walt Whitman, once said. My Soul has appeared; I am saying these words with all my heart. It is beautiful to be alive. I wish for your breathing, laughing, loving, and being. What else can I want for you?

The moments of this universal love are the treasures I collect every day in the garden of my life. These moments make me write and tell you about the miracle of life. I am the ark in the flood of times. I am here now. I want to tell you about the wonders of being Present. To be a real woman or man is terrific! You will feel your love floating through your veins and saying yes to all the challenges life gives you so that you shall awaken.

I am happy to walk this earth. I am content with my suffering and glad to be here as I say these words. What else can I have in this Moment of my Awakening, this Moment of being alive and happy?

To be awake is to live freely. Everything else is living in the dungeon of one's own making.

At times, I stop and see the flower on the table, the cup

with the steaming coffee, firmly holding it in my hand, feeling the warmth, smelling the aroma of the dark roast, and my hands lifting it to my lips. It is beautiful to be Present. Life is happening now; I am free, a man who is a human God.

And then there is darkness. I open my email account and read an email. My bank account has an overdraft fee. I ignore the message. The next one says a subscription fee is due in three days, and I must pay $49.99. Next, my renters tell me that the heating is not working and that I might have to install a new heating system.

I am lost at this point. I am defeated and overrun by the many thoughts that govern life. Where is the flower? Do I see my hands holding an enticing hot cup of coffee? It is gone with the wind. My Presence was short-lived. I am vowing not to be swept away so quickly next time. Next time, there will be other problems and identifications, and I am again angry with self-pity and confusion.

Our lives will unfold this way many times. I am tired of it. The beginning of your inner journey starts when all these human identifications drain you. I wake up and see my life in its many challenging ways. I wake up and cannot close my eyes anymore to the need for suffering as the incubator of change. I will tell you my story in this book so you can live yours. Your story is the only one that matters. It is, after all, your Awakening.

You will need to face the brutal realities of your life on the road to Awakening. The details might differ, but the main obstacles are the same: Negative Emotions, *Identification**, and *Imagination**. So, join me on this path and let go of the shackles that bound you to misery and despair.

I have written this book with the understanding that you and I are traveling the same road, the *"Road for Traveling Souls."* There is nothing else to speak of or reason to linger behind. Do you see yourself now? What are you manifesting?

"Just to stand up with presence is liberation." Robert Burton

"I see you lurking." Walt Whitman

My Story is Your Story

~

"Very little is needed to make a happy life; it is all within yourself in your way of thinking." Marcus Aurelius

My Art is to Be Here Now. I tune my instrument for Awakening in the morning. I prepare my canvas and arrange the colors I will use for the day. I am the artist of my life. This life is lovely and unique, and I am the one who writes my story today, every day. I awake in the morning, thanking the Gods for my appearance. I read poetry or inspirational thoughts instead of the newspapers I did for a long time. I was a journalist for many years, hooked to the news because I had to know what was happening worldwide. I was bombarded with negativity, caught by grim headlines, and angered by politics.

. . .

Now I only know what is going on inside of me. The power of the headlines is gone, and I drink my hot cup of coffee to the words of Conscious Beings, who invite me to share their journey. The beautiful flower on my table also asks me for attention. I am amazed by the simple beauty of life when the morning light shines through my window, awakening me to my *Higher Self**.

Like you, I am trying to be present in my life. It is a beautiful journey that we are taking. No vacation, though. I applaud your efforts; I cherish your suffering, I am you, and you are me while on this journey.

"You will find me under your boot-soles," Walt Whitman shouts in My Awakening Self. Tears are running down my cheeks. Not the tears of self-pity or suffering, but the tears of joy and happiness to be alive, to have found the meaning of life, to being just here is plentiful. Finally, I can say all these words without hesitance or deceit.

Be Present with me right now. Feel the book in your hand; the joy of Awakening your Soul. To "Be" is enough. I am telling you about this wondrous world, your richness, and the joy in your life. But the only true gift I can give you is this Moment now; take it, cherish it, love it. Nothing else matters in this life. It is yours only.

"Remember you are not a crow, but the mystic osprey that never needs to light" is Rumi's thought I recite in the morning. I know I am, and I hope you understand your purpose and mission with my humble words throughout this book.

As of now, I am sitting in my office in Northern California. Reflecting on my life, I see missed opportunities, failed ventures, naivety, and too much imagination. But all mistakes and shortcomings are what brought me to this point. Without them, I would not be able to see and understand. Before, I dreamed of making a difference in the world. Now, I know I can make only a difference in myself.

Since being a journalist in Germany in the 1980s and 1990s, I witnessed many changes in me and the world, experiencing the fall of the Soviet Union and the reunification of Germany. I was part of it, close by, reporting the wall's fall, people coming to the West, and being amazed by capitalism's material riches. Wealth and material goods are the idols of sleeping people. They imagine a meaningful life is to dine in expensive restaurants, have the latest iPhone, or own a villa at sea.

People place so much importance on ownership of things. Their mental illusion of wealth has blocked the understanding of Being as the only actual possession in life.

The mind craves to identify with material objects. People imagine that their wealth reflects their being. Only in the face of death will they understand that ownership is meaningless.

Most spiritual traditions ask to renounce all possessions as the starting point to freeing your ego *(lower self*)* from the material world. But giving up your possessions will not automatically make you free from them. The *lower self** ensures survival by shifting identification to other aspects of your existence. The feeling of being unique, having given up the material world, the superiority to others by living a spiritual life, or the strong perception of right or wrong are all elements of the ego. We can call this part in us also 'false personality,' displaying the impulses of our lower nature, the habitual negative emotions, and resentments, the shell without any substance.

The content of your ego may change, but the structure remains in place: good and evil, right or wrong. The ego lives through comparison. The way people see you is the way you perceive yourself. Wanting to be seen as more spiritual is the same as showing off wealth and fame. It makes no difference. It is just a different stage, a different performance.

Material wishes are not foreign to me; they are part of human life. You can have a life full of comfort and possessions if you want. However, you cannot identify with it. So, enjoy the gifts of this world, but do not hang onto them. No U-Haul truck will follow behind your hearse.

How difficult is it to become a Conscious Being, and how easy is it to make a lot of money? If you want it, it is within your reach. Do it, and be present while you are doing it! Enjoy your worldly gifts, share them with the less fortunate, and remember that everything can be taken away from you anytime.

Instead, allow yourself to be human and create the God within you. I believe in making the New Man and harmonizing with this world. It is beautiful to appear.

Love penetrates everything; love is eternal and is all we

need to remember. This book shall remind you about your Awakening. Nothing else matters; nothing is more important. So, let's travel this road together.

As we walk together, know that I try to be present but still reel in the aftermath of the battle I had this morning. My mind is sometimes a wild boar fighting at every disturbance. And yet the time I spend going into the dungeon becomes less violent. I am guided by *Higher Forces** (Angels, God, a Higher Power), and they let me see my foolishness.

In the morning, I recite these words: "I release the burden of my resentment to my *Higher Self** and go free and happy!"

I say these words and try to feel them. But how difficult is it to feel anything? Isn't love an instant feeling? Isn't hate an instant sense of negativity? How can I create a positive attitude that leads me to Heaven instead of the misery of my inner hell?

The only answer I have found and will tell you about is To Be in the Moment. This understanding is the beginning of change.

I am trying to give up my resentment, programming, and pain, yet I still carry so much baggage from growing up in an impoverished household. I wanted to live like my classmates whose fathers were rich and powerful. The same thought patterns and attitudes still haunt me today, although I am now a grown man creating my own life.

Whatever it is in your life, it is correct. It is a simple sentence to write but a revelation to understand. You are what you are supposed to Be. What freedom! Say this sentence: I am the woman I am! Be it, feel it, suffer it. This is the basis of Awakening.

> *"A good man does nothing for the sake of appearance but for the sake of doing right." Epictetus*

The Art to Be Here Now

~

"We specialize in simply being where we are." Robert Burton

The Art of Being Here Now is not an attempt to improve your thinking, speaking, or doing things more efficiently. These are human functions and belong to a different world.

To be an artist, you don't have to compose music, paint, be in the movies, or write books. Instead, it is in the way you live your life. It involves paying attention to your surroundings, being aware of your actions, understanding the meaning of your life, and experiencing it fully. This is the Art to Be Here Now.

This new way of thinking is Spiritual Consciousness realized and emotionally expressed through Conscience. No aspect of us is more puzzling than Consciousness. The experience of our Soul in this world is our only actual possession.

In the academic world, Consciousness is an elusive concept. Originally it was derived from the Latin con (with) and scire (to know). Through Consciousness, one can understand the external world or one's mental state. Scientists and Philosophers have tried and are still trying to answer what Consciousness is. Where is it located? Does it appear and disappear? Is it a human illusion? What benefit does it have, and can we live without it?

Science sees Consciousness as the biggest mystery of the human brain. They are baffled by our subjective experience of the world and all its perceptual contents, including sights, sounds, thoughts, and sensations. They do not understand this private inner universe that utterly disappears in states such as general anesthesia or dreamless sleep. Science calls it so mysterious that nobody seems to understand or be able to define it.

In the last few years, neurologists at Harvard Medical School have been convinced that our Consciousness sits in a particular part of our brain, precisely in our brainstem, a central axis connecting our cerebrum (Latin for "brain") to our spinal cord and cerebellum (Latin for "little brain").

The Harvard researchers found this area by studying the part of the brain that ceases to operate for comatose or vegetative patients.

But this is not the Consciousness I am talking about. This research shows the central gap between science, spirituality, knowledge, and Soul.

Science does not understand the Consciousness of being connected to one's *Higher Self**. They mistake Consciousness for something that differentiates somebody from a person in a vegetative state, people with brain trauma, people in a coma, or the like, versus regular folks who can talk, move, or think.

The Consciousness we are working for can be called Spiritual Consciousness. It is being able to do everything regular people do but Being Present while doing it. It is impossible to tell people about this. It is something unique to work for and make efforts to achieve. In their mind, individuals believe they already possess it. But you know what I truly mean. You also feel the difference; therefore, you are reading this book. You experienced your Soul, *and* now you long for more Conscious Moments. This is the beginning of your Journey to Presence and your true identity, the difference between longing for an actual existence and not being satisfied with sleep.

Spiritual Consciousness, the realization of one's *Higher Self**, is our true identity. Nothing compares to it. These experiences have the characteristic of simplicity. It is a song without words, a deathless state, a place of our sanity.

To make it permanent, we must be consistent in our efforts. Naïve enthusiasm only lasts for some time. We need to replace our indifference with realizing that we exist only when present. Therefore, we must have a total commitment to Awakening. It is the most challenging undertaking in anybody's life. Imagine the stories of the Conscious Beings in humanity's history, their suffering, labor, and divine guidance.

Our stories will bring us to Awakening, our divine art form. It is simple, such as seeing the beauty of a flower or the clouds in the sky, tasting a morsel of food, sensing your feet on the ground while walking, or embracing your beloved with the gentle sweetness of your love.

This Moment is all we have, the eternal fountain of life, always here, attainable, achievable, ready to be experienced. No more excuses.

You hold this book in your hand. Feel it, read it with the awareness of how you sit, how the light falls through the window. I am writing these words, knowing that nothing else matters. So many people love to read inspirational thoughts but never realize that it is not the reading that matters; it is only understanding and doing that makes the difference.

You can pick up on this energy. Do it now and realize your incredible journey into Being. This book is not a book; it is a calling to your *Higher Self**. So please do not read further, be here now, feel your life, your existence, whatever it is. You are here. You are the artist of your life. So, make it a beautiful painting, a song to remember, a poem to recite, a gentle dance.

Start now. It does not matter how small your effort is. It is the beginning of your new life. Arrange something in your room to make it more beautiful to gaze at; go outside and smell a flower or walk right through the streets with a child's awareness as you view your neighborhood for the first time. The tree is blooming, the neighbor is watering her lawn, and the children are running after the ice cream truck.

One may understand something today and not comprehend it tomorrow because Consciousness has degrees. Try to understand more fully that you are asleep if you are not Here Now. Be repelled by sleep and grow your desire to awaken.

When one does not have Consciousness, one quietly disappears, robbed by the *lower self** and rapped into *imagination** and *identification**.

To achieve this Consciousness, you must first know yourself, and then you can Be yourself. Break through the veil of imagination. Complex events and friction are needed to lift this veil. So accept whatever is given to you.

You might find out later that these experiences are the best things in your life. This concept is hard to believe, but they will change you, nurse you, and force you to grow up. Could you live it now?

There is nothing else besides Being Present in this life we have. It might be limited by money, clouded by a recent divorce, and full of physical pain. It might be full of excitement for the new job or joy to be accepted into your dream college. It makes no difference. It comes and goes. Nothing is permanent besides your Moments of Presence. This is your life. Please don't waste it by daydreaming. You can grab it with the assurance of being alive to anything that comes your way.

Consciousness is the key to your longing. People are usually not conscious, but only in rare moments when something extraordinary happens to them. Later, these moments are called memories. How much remembrance do we generally create in our life? What did we have for lunch on Tuesday? What did we do last Sunday evening?

Does anybody know? Let's start right now. We begin at this Moment. I write this sentence on my keyboard with Presence; I see my fingers going over the keys. How can I tell you about the joy of Awakening and Being Present while writing this sentence? You will understand once you make this Moment your own harbor and destination.

Make Presence Your Destination. Nothing else matters. Not your job, your money, or your achievements. Be here now with me. I am telling you my story of Awakening. Write your own story.

The incidents and experiences in our life are behind a thick veil because we lack Consciousness. Be more awake, live in the Present, and be the conscious actor in your story.

Everything you ever wanted starts on the other side of sleep.

. . .

The steps in our journey to reach the other side will always lead us in one direction. The landscape might change, and the people you linger with might differ, but our efforts are always the same. Sense yourself taking a breath, see your hands moving, hear your voice. See the light, look somebody in their eyes, listen to their words, and be kind to them. Forgive them when they insult you, offer them your assistance, love them, cherish them, and wish them all the best on their journey.

Are you aware of holding this book in your hands? Do you feel its weight and texture? Do you see the words popping up from the background of this page? Do you hear the noise around you?

Do you sense your feet on the ground, your breath, your thoughts?

Being aware of oneself is Spiritual Consciousness. I will only talk about this. Not about some philosophical or neuroscience theory, but your life and how it unfolds from Moment to Moment.

Do not let your life slip into nothingness through daydreaming, fear, and negativity.

Do not fear your death but fear not having lived at all.

"We are always on the same internal journey, no matter where we are." Robert Burton

Awakening – The Eternal Mystery

~

"Many simply do not have the courage to bear Presence and prefer absence." Rumi

Consciousness has appeared and stayed when you awaken to your *Higher Self**. The Awareness of yourself, the realization of "I am," can last for seconds, minutes, or hours.

Awakening has degrees. It differs in duration, meaning how long you can stay Conscious. In frequency, how often are you Present, and in-depth, how deeply do you experience your Awareness?

Awakening is a process, and you reach your Awareness more frequently and with greater intensity by making efforts. Therefore, when you are present, your Spiritual Consciousness appears.

· · ·

Your Awakening brings you closer to understanding what Spiritual Consciousness means. It is your experience to see the mind thinking, to sense your body's experience, and to understand your interactions with the world and its people.

Consciousness is not part of it, though. It exists separate from all our perceptions, sensations, and experiences.

Consciousness is always there, but we fall asleep to it. We become identified with our mind and body and lose the connection. The attention leaves Awareness, and the experiences of our body, mind, and the world become blurred. Then we are separated from experiencing sensations, thoughts, and perceptions objectively.

We are caught in the net of *identification** and *imagination** that denies us from grasping the meaning of our life.

Let me explain what I understand about *identification** and *imagination**.

These are terms used in the System of the Fourth Way, the teachings of George Gurdjieff and Peter Ouspensky.

Identification is a major obstacle to experiencing Spiritual Consciousness. It stands in the way of seeing ourselves and the world as it is. We are losing ourselves in one aspect of life; our attention is only concentrated on one topic, one incident, one occurrence. It is easy to see the identification of people with sports teams, celebrities, or political parties, but identification happens every moment when we are not present. We are identified when traffic is heavy, being in a hurry. We are identified as going to the movies and not seeing and perceiving anything else until the lights go on again. We are lost in front of the computer or cell phone and forget anything else around us. Identification is sleep.

The sleeping world asks us to identify with all the glamour or despair around us. We have ceased to exist.

Imagination is daydreaming, the uncontrolled activities in our head. We believe things about ourselves that are not true. We imagine ourselves. We assume powers and qualities that do not exist. Our imagination displaces reality. In our imagination, there is always a tomorrow until there is no more tomorrow.

Chet Baker's song comes into my mind: "Imagination is so funny it makes a rainy day sunny." Sure, imagining sunshine instead of rain might be nice, but Awakening means seeing things as they are and not as I wish them to be.

Outside Consciousness, there is no objective experience. Choose to awaken instead.

To awaken is to come home. We awaken from our deep sleep and understand the purpose of our existence.

To awaken is to see things as they are. No more lies and false idols, just the appearance of God in human form, experiencing one's true Self.

To awaken is to connect to the universal Consciousness that exists beyond any physical and mental identity. To awaken is to lift the veil from our eyes and realize that this world is not separated but united by love and light.

The first time I woke up, a light came on. I did not see with my eyes anymore but through my eyes. I appeared apart from my body and mind. My Being was revealed. It had been waiting long and patiently to come into existence.

After some time, this *Higher State** disappeared, and I fell back into my usual state of sleep. But the experience of Being Present changed my life. This Moment of understanding installed a longing that never ceased to guide me.

My story of Awakening is a simple one—nothing to brag about. An ordinary man is connecting with his *Higher Self**, his Soul. Nothing has externally changed, just an awareness of myself that will never cease.

Nobody notices my Awareness. How could they? I have nothing to show besides my humble appearance while I view the world around me a little brighter. However, I am aware of my body when I awaken. Human functions do not automatically happen anymore without me noticing them. I have an awareness that does not cease. The veil has been lifted. I observe this man, Klaus Labuttis, and sometimes wonder about his habits. I am amazed by his thoughts and amused by his feelings. He is a good man with all the usual faults one can find in anybody, with no unique gifts or capabilities more than the average man.

I am glad that he is inconspicuous and unimportant. He longs for coffee, dark and bold coffee in the morning. He thinks he is too fat and typically does intermittent fasting. He is very particular when brushing and flossing his teeth; his style of clothing is vibrant, although his meager income does not allow for anything extravagant and designer outfits.

I am aware of his *lower self**. His ego is a net of recurring thoughts and emotions that gives him a false identification and an imaginary idea of who he thinks he is.

The *lower self**, ego or false personality exists in all people as an imaginary picture of oneself. It is protected with all kinds of psychological mechanisms to sustain this image. It developed since early childhood and grew into a socially accepted role, displaying a network of attitudes and patterns that are just learned and acquired without any true nature of who one really is.

Though I am aware that I am thinking, my Consciousness has nothing to do with this thinking. The capability to think is just a function that some people have developed better than others. It is like tasting food or smelling a fragrance. Some people can do it better than others. It is their mechanics. Although one can train and sophisticate these skills, they are also given at birth. How can one be proud of something that is given and not earned? Being Conscious is achieved. Being Present is spiritual work that separates the sleeper from the sage, the machine from a God.

Consciousness is the perception that "I am" separate from my body and mind. Therefore, I will survive my physical death.

Perceiving our identity is Consciousness itself and not our ego or the *lower self**. Somebody cannot give this to you; it must be earned and experienced. There is no form attached to our Being. The ultimate truth of who we are is not what we possess or think but the perception of "I am."

Typically, people are identified with the voice in their head. This voice wraps them into their identifications, judgments, and opinions. People are unaware of this. They believe that these expressions are who they are. Their mind is stamped with the seal of sleep, the illusions of form and matter. No understanding can occur in this state of mind.

The ego thrives in judgment and complaints. So often, these identifications lead to aggressive forms of shouting, name-calling, and even physical violence—king of the jungle.

I have understood that my words and doings result in creating my world. I am responsible for my life, and every slip of the tongue or resentment I feel will set me back in my grasp for gaining more Consciousness and Presence.

I know I am a beginner. I have started to be present, but I understand that many higher levels of existence are still hidden. I am a toddler who has started to walk, but it is a long way to start dancing.

As I continue on my journey, every day, I formulate specific aims to accomplish throughout my day to stay focused on retaining Presence. I am opening doors by seeing and sensing my hand pushing down the handle. I take my time, even if it means arriving late to an appointment. Smiling at the people I meet and listening when they speak to me—eating slowly, tasting the sandwich. My day is filled with these little reminders of my Presence, showing me that nothing is more important than to be in the Moment.

. . .

Finally, I understand that all my efforts are the preparation for my final Awakening. In this lifetime, my *Higher Self** might permanently fuse and appear. I do not know nor worry. I am on my way to immortality, living my own story, my myth. It is a story of many missed opportunities and mistakes, but this is also a crucial part of it.

Create Your Own Story. The only one worth telling in this world is your Awakening story. It is possible once you let go of the *identifications** and *imaginations** that govern your life.

Wake Up! Now is the time.

*"No single event can awaken within us a stranger totally unknown to us. To live is to be slowly born. It would be a bit too easy if we could go about borrowing ready-made souls." Antoine de Saint-*Exupéry

The Story of Creating a Mirror

~

A holy person lived far away from everybody, not taking on students or accepting followers. He just lived his life following high moral standards and observations for the gods. One day a young man shows up at the humble dwelling of this conscious man, asking him to be allowed to meditate in his Presence and receive his bliss. The sage agreed, although he told the young man that he had nothing to offer besides his simple life and his care for his animals' well-being, which, in turn, fed him and provided a meager income by selling milk and cheese to the nearby village.

So, the young man sat beside the sage in his yoga lotus position, closed his eyes, and pronounced the word OM to himself. After some time, the young man heard stones rubbing against each other and opened his eyes. He saw the sage rubbing two ordinary pebbles against each other. He asked: "Master, what are you doing, rubbing these stones together?" The holy man replied, "I am rubbing them to create a mirror."

"But Master, this will never happen," said the young man. "These are just two ordinary pebbles that will never be shiny enough to become a mirror."

"Exactly," responded the master. "Therefore, you will never reach Nirvana by sitting in a yoga position with closed eyes. Awakening is living a life of high moral standards that do not pretend or show."

Memories

~

"I'm beginning to get used to regarding death and dying not as the end of my task but as the task itself." Leonid Tolstoy

Where are my childhood memories? The early years of my life have been erased from my memory. They are behind a thick veil of imagined events and stories without remembrance. Reflected in a few surviving photos, they do not trigger within me any emotional response.

The only event I can recall vividly from childhood is when I came home from the hospital on my tenth birthday. I spent two weeks in an orthopedic clinic to remove a benign tumor in my right elbow. Although the surgery was successful, it left my right arm partially handicapped—a blow to my aspirations of becoming a successful Handball player. My mother picked me up on a beautiful spring day on the 31st of May, and we even drove by taxi – a seldom luxury – back home. My father, awaiting my return, proudly gave me a self-made table tennis plate. I can still see his face gleaming with joy at the sight of my excitement. My mother prepared fresh strawberries from our garden to combine with ice cream, and I felt so happy.

This birthday was one of my rare moments of being present as a child. Children should remember many moments of their existence, a well full of joy to reminisce about for when they have become old with short-term memory loss and worn down by life's disappointments.

But where are my memories? Seeing a dog for the first time, a rose, the sound of thunder, and the red colors of a sunset? A psychiatrist might explain my lack of memories from almost drowning in a rainwater barrel in my parent's garden. Therefore, my mind shut down all events and experiences in my life. I do not know.

When people talked about their numerous experiences during childhood, I felt cheated. I did not feel this deep inner source of joy and bliss. The lack of memories and vividly experienced moments became one of the driving forces in my search for the meaning of life.

Even growing into adolescence, I gained only a few more memories. Spread over months and years, it seemed that life only happened in these short polaroid instances. Everything else seemed to be just a vegetative existence without importance.

. . .

While writing these words, I remember some parts of my early life. The embarrassment of seeing the dirty fingernails of my father while he attended my Handball game and sadly leaving after I pointed out his negligence. My mother's beatings because I missed an important exam. I fled into the bathroom, locking myself away from her thrashing hands. My memories are filled chiefly with pain and suffering, the shortcomings of a simple boy wanting to be more than just a puppet with regular life expectations and aims.

Sadly, it is dull to say that my first memories were primarily dark and painful events. Do I recall making love for the first time? Do I remember my first achievement of creating a drawing, a kite, or a sandcastle? Unfortunately, no, and this is the beginning of my story.

During my young adult years, I became a junkie for extreme events, traveling to dangerous and unique places to feel a little bit more real, to have some moments to pocket, and some experiences that would linger on beyond a short flash. Drugs and alcohol became other tools in my daily kit to becoming more aware, not understanding that these toxins prevented me from actually experiencing my life.

In my foolish attempt at creating memories, I became successful. I became a man searching for a higher purpose, trying to feel anything that appeared authentic.

My first homosexual experiences as a sixteen-year-old boy with an older man in Paris as we excessively drank champagne; my hitchhike through Holland in Winter and ending up in a homeless shelter; my venture to sell Mercedes Benz vehicles in civil-war-torn Lebanon, waiting at the border while mortars were falling close by. Seducing my substitute teacher at a school party, traveling Europe via rail, and cooking on a gas stove in the rail compartments. Stealing bread from a bakery in Greece, storming into a famous Restaurant in Paris shouting "bourgeois, bourgeois!" with my like-minded socialist friends, and then later making love to one of the women activists.

Now I know that these were all expressions of a seeking soul, a soul in the making, a man destined to become Conscious but needing to take his first steps blind and without any clues.

Now I know that these early experiences were necessary preparations for what has come into my life. My childhood embarrassment of being overweight, my fear of being poor, and my anxiety about the prospects in my life.

I felt lost; I felt like somebody not worth being alive. Yet, this pain and suffering were necessary to cast me into the man I am today—the man who understands that suffering is the ingredient for love, for Awakening. Knowing you went through similar processes and fires, I want to share my gift. I am here. You are here.

Let's celebrate our Awakening.

"Can you remember the present?" Rumi

Humble Beginnings

∾

"Hang on to your youthful enthusiasm; you'll be able to use them better when you're older." Seneca

I was standing in front of a 1950s grey apartment building in Wedding, West-Berlin, a working-class neighborhood, on an icy cold November evening just minutes before 8 p.m.

Here was supposedly the Berlin Center for a School to Awaken. Awakening was a lofty concept for me at the time, and it was an idealized connection that I made on my travels to India, Nepal, and Thailand. A new beginning to grasping Spiritual Consciousness, not with chemical help but by using techniques and efforts to create this state on my own.

· · ·

Here I was on this freezing evening, the 22nd of November 1984, and judging by the location, a relatively meager venue for my search for eternal bliss and Consciousness.

I had come a long way since my first marihuana joint after school with my charismatic friend, Michael, who introduced me to all kinds of mind-altering substances, from LSD to Psilocybin.

At this time, I was fascinated with astrology, practiced it for myself, and made charts and interpretations for others. These were moments of vanity and psychological children's games, taking advantage of people's naivety who were fascinated by somebody who could read their past and presumably their future.

I was practicing a specific astrological system that was centered around the cycles of the Sun and the Moon. The Sun is the principle of our actions and what we express and give in life. Starting at the Ascendent, one moves every ten years along the Houses from first to second, third to fourth, and so on. Consider the Sign that governs the specific House and its ruling Planet, and look where this interaction unfolds and what other elements are involved. To calculate the event's timeframe, one divides the degrees of the specific House by ten, and each increment represents one year.

The calculations must go the opposite direction when looking at the Moon, representing our inner world and feelings. So, again, one starts from the Ascendant, but this time in the order of the 12th House to the 11th House, and so on, each House lasts for seven years. Then, depending on the Sign and the Planet governing the House, one can calculate what was deeply emotional to this person at different times.

It is a mind-boggling science that I still use from time to time to see what happens in my life, being curious about what I need to face with my Conscious mind right now.

Taking my example, having an Ascendant of Cancer with the Sun, Venus, and Mercury all populating the 12th House, this knowledge allows me to see specific incidents happening in my early childhood from zero to seven years of age. For example, drowning almost in a rain barrel was evident with a conjunction of the Moon (ruler of Cancer) with Uranus in the Third House. At three years old, this explosive experience became active when the dreadful incident of almost drowning occurred.

So, I could tell people about their past and future with this knowledge. I was a star astrologer in my first years in West Berlin, making and interpreting charts of famous people in this surreal town, a hotbed for all kinds of unique people. We all wanted to be different from what the traditional German society offered. So, we came to West Berlin to chase our dreams and aspirations.

As I stepped before the school's front door, I rang the bell at precisely 8 p.m. and was asked to come up to the 4th floor, where a well-dressed middle-aged man opened the door. The apartment was simple but elegant, and many prints of classical paintings hung on the walls. I still vividly remember the beautiful, clean wine glass filled with water offered to me and how my perception of its beauty caused an awareness within me.

My so-called "prospective student meeting" covered the lies people tell themselves about being present, having no will, or unity. In addition, I was introduced to a technique called "Dividing Attention," which could lead to Spiritual Consciousness, called "Self-Remembering."

Self-Remembering and Dividing Attention are the cornerstones in the "Fourth Way" to grow spiritually. This ancient system of inner development was rediscovered by George Gurdjieff and, with the help of his most important student, Peter Ouspensky, popularized.

Self-Remembering is the realization of our Soul, the completion of our existence, the creation of memory, and the connection to the universal Consciousness around us. Our *Higher Self* * appears; we are Present in the Here and Now.

Dividing Attention is the technique of being aware of two things simultaneously. We are looking at an object or listening to a sound, and at the same time, we experience ourselves doing it. We are aware of our environment and, at the same time, of ourselves in it. By Dividing our Attention, Self-Remembering can emerge.

This meeting took place almost four decades ago, and I have studied and practiced the tools to awaken that were given to me over the years by my teacher Robert Burton. Being close to him at times and experiencing his love and Presence has guided me ever since.

Now, it is time for me to give my understanding and offer my Being to You, dear Reader. Nothing is more beautiful than To Be Here Now.

My Presence is unfolding and has become my permanent companion. I have doubted myself for a long time, feeling unworthy of the gift bestowed on me. Now I can tell you the truth of my Awakening, and this book expresses my path. Your Awakening is waiting for you as well. It starts now with the remembrance of your Soul, the realization of where you are, and the love you feel for all the people you meet— good or bad. They are neither your friends nor enemies but only your teachers.

I would like to share with you my story of Awakening. I want to show you some of the tools I have discovered and the teachings I came across that helped me better understand myself. My lessons were challenging, as they must be to make a difference. Do not imagine that Awakening is easy. You need to suffer. It would be best if you felt your despair to wake up. The highest achievement of Awakening was shown to us by Jesus Christ and his suffering on the cross. We are suffering on our own cross; it feels horrible, and the pain is excruciating and endless. But this is the fire you need to have. Can you achieve excellence without suffering? People study for hours to prepare for exams and suffer through ordeals to be recognized for their achievements.

Nobody will remember you for your achievements of being Present.

To them, it means nothing in this world. But you know this means everything. So do not be discouraged; understand and go the way of your liberation.

. . .

But please, do not be satisfied with my story and what I tell you. You know it now yourself. You can unfold your myth; be the woman present in her life. Please do not allow anybody to question your mission. Sleeping people want to destroy us by identifying with life's values: the house, the car, the vacation, and the money in the bank. I show you treasures beyond your imagination. Turn around what life tells you to pursue, be different, and be here now.

The world will change in front of your eyes.

"The path to Paradise begins in Hell." Dante Alighieri

Spiritual Consciousness - Being Present

~

"Nothing is more exciting than being present to your own life." Robert Burton

To Be Present is the greatest miracle in life. Everything begins and never ends from our Awakening. It is a simple, eternal story: to be where one is, accept, understand, and appear. When one is present, one pierces eternity.

Consciousness is that in which all our experiences appear and are made. Through Consciousness, all of our experiences are known. Consciousness is ever-present and without limits. It is infinite; it knows itself in itself and by itself. We must see our reality to understand the universe's reality.

Each moment allows us to be present in it. We need to shift our aim towards to Be instead of to do. Events causing friction and pain can force us into our Presence. Please do not waste your suffering in self-pity and anger but use it for your Soul to appear. Our efforts to Be in the Moment become self-defense instead of self-pity, accepting what had to happen and realizing that we always make a profit.

Being Present is our Home. The place we can always return to and be loved. Whatever the present offers us is our task at hand. Be grateful for it. Refrain from imagining something coming along that may carry more excellent value. As Walt Whitman said: *"The insignificant is as big to me as any."*

Time is swift, and even living to old age appears like a moment. People think they have time to be present or believe it is designed for exceptional circumstances. Refrain from falling into the trap of mechanical life that wants to permeate your Presence with minor things. Instead, prolong your life by calling today your own. Only the Moments you were present are yours; everything else has gone into oblivion. To Be Here Now is the definition of our success. It is the only currency recognized in Paradise. Our lives are comprised of these moment-to-moment struggles. These struggles will lead to Presence.

Only our Presence is real. Everything else is an illusion designed to keep us asleep.

The *lower self** in us opposes our Awakening. It is happy to have you asleep. Glad to be in control by dangling the poisonous fruits of worldly goods before your eyes. Success, money, power, influence— all these short-lived pleasures of human life. This part in you is an obvious absurdity that thinks it is profound.

. . .

We all have been cast into a complicated situation, and the answer is quite simple: To Be Present.

Our ego wants our life to be exciting, eventful, and full of friends and activities. So, the places to choose are the loud temples of pleasure, the bars and restaurants, the event parties, and the public gatherings.

We all have the superficial satisfaction of being recognized on social media or the eventful nothingness of being surrounded by familiar strangers whose goals and aspirations differ from ours.

Our sleeping self is strong and tries to hold us hostage to its aims and aspirations. But there is a great secret that you can have both. You can be successful in this life and at the same time be not attached to your achievements and successes. You do not need to be poor. You do not need to give up life's beauty to become Conscious. You can have it all. The Bible says that *"the love of money is the cause of all evil."* Do not love money; enjoy what it is giving you. Enjoy the beauty of a wealthy lifestyle and understand that it can be taken away from you at any time. It is a gift that can and will perish. Love it, enjoy it, and be ready to give it up.

Deviations, like money, are essential. Experiencing this empty glamour and being fed up with its superficial reward is the first step toward Awakening.

Being lost, disappointed, and tired of striving for outside acceptance is vital for inner evolution. Waking up to the reality of life and one's worldly fascinations is the starting point in anybody's spiritual journey.

While reflecting on my inner search, one of my favorite poems was "The Departure of the Prodigal Son" by the German poet Rainer Maria Rilke. He was one of the artists whose work was part of his spiritual journey. So likewise, we can use the writings, paintings, and music of Conscious Beings to inspire our efforts and find a supportive element in our daily struggles to be present.

Rilke says:

> *"... And still to go, hand ripped from hand*
> *as if from something healed, now newly torn.*
> *Go where? Into the far-away, forlorn*
> *uncertainty of some warm, static land*
> *that, like the backdrop to all scenes, is worn,*
> *a wall indifferent, a garden bland.*
> *To go: but why? From need or disposition?*
> *Impatience or some darkening premonition?*
> *Misunderstood? Failing to understand?*
> *To take all this upon yourself, to drop*
> *things held (perhaps in vain), so you can die*
> *alone — alone and yet not knowing why:*
> *Is this the beginning of a new life?"*

This "going" is and must be painful. We do not know what awaits us on the other side, but we no longer have a choice. There is no way back when you start to awaken and begin seeing reality as it is. Uneasiness and restlessness have started within you. Life tastes like champagne opened long ago, and the sparkling bubbles have faded.

You cannot overpower the stale taste of your old life with more fun, materialistic things or anything external.

Our new life awaits; it is optional for our journey's scenery. It can be in the cloisters of the Himalayas or the busy office on Main Street. It does not matter. Your spiritual journey is happening inside you; no external stimuli or exterior canvas must be created to make this leap.

Are there no circumstances better than others for Awakening?

I do not know. However, your circumstances were designed for your life to give you the experiences you need to evolve. So, you don't need to change them but accept them.

Acceptance is our primary guide while on this path. Acceptance is the pill we take when the going gets rough. Acceptance is not the helpless cry of despair but the power inside us to change our Being.

Accepting whatever comes your way is the beginning of our New Life.

How do I long for acceptance in my life? I fight any misadventure, any wrongdoing, any suffering. When will I understand that this is part of Awakening? You want something, which is denied, so you behave like a toddler, erupting with cries and wails.

The stoic philosophers, primarily the Conscious Beings Marcus Aurelius and Epictetus, focus on understanding what is in our control instead of behaving irrationally. It is not the event by itself but our attitude and interpretation of what is happening. What we see depends on our perspective; it is not the truth, only how we view it. Any distress we are experiencing, and the pain connected with it, is not caused by the thing itself but by our viewpoint. You can change this attitude at any time.

You want to wake up, right? Be a woman, a man, live up to the challenges in your life, and do not complain about other people, the sun not shining, or the rain pouring down on you. When you realize your aim, everything is a tool, a means to achieve excellence; everything is helping you to Be. Be Present right now. What choice do you have?

We all have our buffers, our blind spots in life—the explanations for why we cannot do something right now, the excuses that keep us asleep. Now is the time to wake up. It does not take any money to Be Present in what you are doing. You are eating out of a can or a sophisticated meal prepared by a chef; it does not matter. If you do not taste the food, feel the fork in your hand, or see the plate or your hand coming up to your mouth, it all means nothing. Food for sleeping people is only essential to satisfy their hunger. Gourmets die the same as paupers; there is no difference.

"The presence is the only reality." Marcus Aurelius

Divided Attention

~

"Remain here and stay awake with me." Jesus Christ

D iding Attention is staying awake. Beautiful things happen directly before us, but we miss them in our waking sleep, *imagination**, and *identification**. Moments of epiphanies and profound insights are lost in our hurry, our mindlessness in autopilot existence.

To retaliate against this existence, know I am not what I observe but what I observe. When you are Present, your Soul looks through your eyes. The development of your *Higher Self** and your conscious faculties depend on your ability to see reality as it is. The existence of your temporary body and mind changes every moment until this earthly vessel is returned to dust.

. . .

Coming into existence requires continuous effort to appear and be in the Moment. We achieve our *Higher States** by dividing our attention. It means to observe oneself doing things, speaking, drinking, walking, reading – all day-to-day activities – and being present while doing them. Look at them as an outside observer does.

I see my fingers pressing keys on the computer keyboard, I feel my feet on the ground, and I see myself formulating my thoughts into words. I am astonished at my Presence; the light has turned on, and I see things clearly now. I have appeared while looking at my body functioning and doing something. Of course, your body will behave as it always does, but it is so exciting to see it, to observe it, and to understand what I am is not this, but something different that can see all this at once.

I am simply here for my ordinary daily life. Nothing special for somebody who does not understand the difference. Something people think they have already achieved. But I know this is the key to Awakening. To see oneself, to observe my movements, sensations, feelings, and thoughts. My Soul appears in the process.

During these moments, I have no preference or denial; all is good and necessary. I remember a Conscious experience at the beach: I walked down the shore, my naked feet feeling the warm, wet sand. My arms dangled by my sides, the wind blew my hair, and a taste of salt was on my lips. I walked, observed myself, looked into the distance, and tried to be present until I reached the next rock sticking out of the waves.

Then I looked for another landmark and did it again. Finally, a beautiful woman approached me, and I lost myself, peering at her body's shape and long brown hair. We smiled as we passed, and it took me a few more seconds to realize my sleeping self. I focused again on the next rock, now trying to listen to the waves and the intent cries from the seagulls.

I woke up an hour later, back in my apartment, realizing I had entirely forgotten myself. Something in my mind had captured my attention at the beach, pushing me into the dreamlike state of anticipated imagination. At that moment, I recalled that I still needed to renew my driver's license, and the deadline for the new essay was tomorrow, which I had yet to finish. These weary thoughts entered my mind and made me forget my feet on the sand and the seagulls' cries.

Awakening is quite simple. We need to come back to this moment again and again. We must know and observe our actions, thoughts, and feelings. How beautiful it is to taste a piece of bread with butter and cheese; how amazing to hold a clear glass of fresh water in my hand, lift it to my mouth and drink the cool liquid, feeling it in my mouth and throat. The simple things become a feast of existence, an opulence of joy.

Any external achievement falls short of the remembrance of one's *Higher Self**. With any expression of resentment or anger, you hurt your Soul. Do not let the 'evil clown' inside you get the upper hand and triumph in destroying your inner peace and harmony.

But do not judge yourself when this happens. It happens to all of us because we are still learning the Art of

Being Here Now, the technique of Being Present. So, we fall, fail, and learn from our identifications, seeing them as what they are: useless expressions of life in sleep.

When we observe ourselves, the reward is in the observation. This is the hidden meaning of life. We need to know ourselves to Be ourselves. Life is designed to take us away from the moment.

Sporting events, shows, and concerts are made to fascinate us, let us identify with the external world, and make us forget our Soul. We all fall into these traps, but soon we start to detect them and avoid them gradually.

You know where your primary identification lies. Is it the daily newspaper consumption with the horrible stories of murders, war, climate change, or injustice? Is it the demanding profession that needs your full attention, working overtime, and the expected identification with corporate sales and profits? Or is it your sports team, Sundays spent on the fields of glory where your cheers and hopes are crashing your awareness?

Whatever it is, try to minimize it. For example, try to understand that eight billion people have similar identifications but do not understand that there is something else in this life: the remembrance of your *Higher Self**, the appearance of your Soul, the Presence within you.

You have the key to eternal life. Dividing your attention and not expressing negative emotions are the foundations of our evolution. When you truly understand that life has nothing to offer, that people are asleep and going nowhere, you have no more time to lose. Every moment counts, and every effort to Be Present is valuable. Do not allow yourself to take breaks from this endeavor. As Jesus Christ pointed out, the son of God has no time to lay his head down. Continue because you must.

The pace quickens for you. The more you try to Be Present, the more you can. Our work is a cumulative process. We build on the foundation of our efforts.

The more upstream you swim in your quest for Awakening, the more complex the current pushes you back. This is the friction and difficulties increasing on your path. They come your way not because you are bad but because they remind you of your aim; they catapult you into Presence when you use them. Accept, let them go, and transform suffering into love and compassion.

We have created eternity when we divide our attention and reach a Moment of Presence. This Moment will not be devoured by death. Instead, we are born again into the glory of our existence; we become the butterfly reborn from its caterpillar state.

Ask only a few questions about how to achieve rebirth. The answer is your *Higher State**, the ability to seize the moment and wake to it. Any time is good to divide your attention.

You know the task at hand. It is a long and challenging road, but the only road worth traveling on. Go from here to here. Make Presence your destination. Look at the things in front of you and look at yourself simultaneously. When you establish the remembrance of yourself in this world, you have discovered the meaning of life. Pursue not the things outside of yourself but inside. When you awake, it becomes more apparent that your hope is aligned with the Gods.

Emperors conquered the world and died alone and with remorse. Conquer yourself, and you will live forever.

"What is essential is invisible to the eye." Antoine de Saint-Exupéry

Painful Awakening

I was horrified when I started to see myself more clearly. It made me unable to find any more excuses or explanations. Seeing myself with new eyes made me shocked about my thoughts, embarrassed by my behaviors, and unsatisfied with my take on life.

Peter Ouspensky - the protagonist of "The Fourth Way," a specific method for Awakening - expresses this perception clearly:

> *"When a man begins to know himself a little, he will see in himself many things that are bound to horrify him. So long as a man is not horrified at himself, he knows Nothing about himself."*

. . .

When one starts to see oneself, the first reactions are to blame and despise oneself. For some seekers, it can lead to depression and fear, and these feelings will often hinder us from going further. Others use their new understanding as a dagger to hurt others by shouting out their superficial revelations.

We all go through different phases within these first steps on the spiritual path. This blaming and judging is common self-defense arising from our *lower self**. The parts of us that do not want to evolve are vital and legion. Refrain from being deceived that your spiritual journey will be a walk in the park, a stroll to gather only beautiful flowers. It is a long, steep pilgrimage, an arduous journey where you sometimes lose your step, fall into the mud, and feel abandoned and misunderstood.

But remember, pain is a purifying fire necessary to cast away the old belief system of right and wrong.

For us, who are walking the path to Consciousness, this realization is the first step on our journey.

I struggle daily to forgive myself for all the negativity and mindlessness that occasionally occurs in me, pushing away my longing for something higher. But this struggle is necessary and good. Because these thoughts and emotions are venoms from the ego, I no longer identify with them. Instead, these destructive voices have become the wake-up call to continue loving me. They are my jumpstart into feeling empowered. They help me focus on the present Moment. We can always make a profit by turning these feelings of despair into our Conscience and Awakening.

At one point, these feelings will become love and compassion.

You cannot be Here Now unless you have love and compassion. So, start with loving and caring for small things, plants and animals, close friends, and family. Eventually, this practice will enable you to go further and spread your love to the people outside your immediate circle.

To be in the Moment is a powerful experience. There is no yesterday or tomorrow; only the Now, the present Moment that exists. I am satisfied with where I am and with what is happening. The longing for a different experience has gone. I am happy to embrace what is given to me.

Why would I want to change it? It is provided to make me Conscious, to remind me about my aim, to help me separate myself from the outside world, and to be thankful for the gift bestowed upon me.

It does not matter anymore if the subway runs late or is overcrowded. I look around, see the people waiting, see the artificial light, smell the musty scent of being underground, and feel the air stirring when the train finally arrives.

It does not matter anymore when somebody drives aggressively and cuts me off. I catch my rising anger; I observe my thoughts and remind myself that I have done similar things, not by intention but by negligence. The driver did not do this to hurt me. So, I forgive and drive on without any resentment.

I accept what is in front of me. My *lower self** loves to complain and be unsatisfied with services or the ordered dish in a restaurant. I used to think this was my sincere expression, something that had to be said about the cold food, the small plate, and the mediocre service. Now I accept it. I am thankful that friction is bringing me back to Myself. The Moment is too precious to smear with negativity disguised as sincere expression. So now I let go and be extra nice to the person who resents me or has a bad day, the ones who are burdened by debts or unreturned love.

It is essential to confront this, to give up this self-righteousness, these assumptions, these made-up convictions. It is crucial to cherish this Moment and not let it slip into negativity or boredom. Our life is comprised of these Moments. The more minuscule they appear, and the more unimportant they seem, the more critical they are for your Awakening. These moments are changing you; they will measure your appreciation and encourage you not to let go of your precious life. Grasp it and live it.

"Serenity comes when you trade expectations for acceptance." The Buddha

Understanding

~

"Very little is needed to make a happy life. It is all within yourself in your way of thinking." Marcus Aurelius

Understanding gives power and confidence to one's efforts to Be Present. Conversely, uncertainty about which efforts to make appears if one lacks understanding.

When our understanding grows, we are more open to conducting experiments and finding new methods to close the gap between one's knowledge and our level of being. When you really start to see and understand, a powerful force has begun which will lead you beyond your comfort zone. This is when the real struggle for Presence begins. The more you understand, the more potent your efforts will become.

When we are in imagination, doubts and fears can enter

our minds and prevent us from understanding reality. We then need to introduce ourselves to some energy to break the chain, like walking in the garden, listening to beautiful music, or reading poetry. Then, when we raise our emotional level, we can connect again with the miraculous.

When we express our understanding concerning our inner evolution, we slowly use simpler and simpler expressions. We have yet to understand as long as we make Awakening and our efforts complicated.

We must purify our thoughts and attitude with the holy water of understanding to bring us there. When the verification comes, it always seems like a miracle is happening. But the slow progress culminates in the eruption of a more profound experience that breaks down the barriers of belief and guesses.

The sum of our verifications leads us to our understanding and gives us the faith to continue our path. These experiences are the only road to God within. All creation is laden with meaning and value.

Everything has a purpose, and figuring that out is part of the story in our Awakening.

I remember the first time I saw my Conscious experiences expressed in movies. They were in a film by a beloved Russian filmmaker, Andrei Tarkovsky, who lived and studied in Berlin for a few years before I arrived. A small movie theater often showed his films, and my friends and I were indeed fans of his work and watched them again and again. There would be a familiar crowd of people, and I often expressed my understanding that Tarkovsky's films are just a reminder to experience what his lens is showing us:

To Be Present.

I remember standing one evening in front of the movie theater before the show began. It was located just opposite a hardcore gay club, and the warm summer evening encouraged the guests to linger outside the entrance, immersed in openly displaying sexual encounters and flirtatious behaviors. Naturally, all the men wore leather outfits.

Everybody was showing off, but I deeply felt the strong disguise of their vulnerability through their fashion, chains, and macho behavior. These moments of waiting and observing enhanced my ability to see and watch the world around me and its meaninglessness. All this was so unreal that my reality appeared.

It was a scenery that could only exist in the Berlin I knew before the wall came down, before the reunification, making it the Capital of united Germany, where it lost all the strangeness and peculiarity that made it so special for us in the early 1980s.

Andrei Tarkovsky's work showed me that other people know about Moments of Presence. As immersed in his films, I understood that I was not alone in seeing simple things as they are in their unique beauty. A willow tree is moving in the wind, a leaf flowing down a small creek, a boy's face smiling vividly, and a hand caressing a friend.

· · ·

His last film gave me an understanding of Consciousness that has filled me with joy through the years. It is called "The Last Sacrifice" and portrays a professor with all the intellectual answers. His philosophical talks are happening without an accurate understanding of the meaning of life. Strangely, the film develops into a plot where nuclear powers threaten the world with war. Finally, the professor stops talking when the atomic war is announced on television. No words can express his horror and disbelief. Words have ceased to make sense, nothing can describe the end of the world and humanity, and his intellectual comments are meaningless in this catastrophe.

I realized what I would do in a moment like this. I would Be Present in the last moments of my life. I would live the remaining moments left awake. A moment like this would be a powerful catalyst to catapult me into the highest state possible for Man. Before my body would perish, my nonperishable Soul would have appeared, carrying me to Paradise.

That movie will be a powerful reminder for my inner work that Awakening is the only aim worth pursuing—the only meaning in my life. I was hooked.

One cannot awaken unless one has verified that one is asleep. What does it mean to understand that one is sleeping?

One can only gain this understanding by trying to be in the Moment. You will notice your lack of trying when you forget to create exercises and reminders to be present throughout your day. Simple activities are helpful, like Being Present when opening and closing doors, being aware of one's thoughts about others, not eating while standing, and reading an inspirational quote after each hour of work.

Having these aims will show you that you forgot. If you are asleep, realize that many things are more important to your *lower self** than Being Present.

By trying to work on yourself, your Being grows, and then your understanding increases. Many people have a lot of knowledge, but they lack understanding. They do not bring their expertise into reality; they are satisfied with words.

To feel real, feel the power inside of you to grasp the Moment and give shape to your world. Nothing will ever be real without beholding it first.

When we start to understand, we become more of who we are daily. Presence does not want to talk about itself; it wants to be itself. Work with esoteric knowledge little by little every day. Reality will start unfolding within you.

Understanding that time is limited will help strengthen one's efforts and help shape our reality. The labor to be in the Moment can never be automatic; it has no momentum on its own. It is always an uphill battle.

You will only reach the top of the hill if you give up your petty convictions and common human beliefs and find the truth by not knowing.

. . .

As Jesus Christ said, to *"become like children to enter the kingdom of heaven,"* we must realize that esoteric wisdom cannot be more than the presence of the child within us. Simple messages reveal what presence indeed is— a conscious child. We are who we are when we achieve the seriousness of a child at play in our work.

Freeing our inner child will enable us to understand that God is simple and loves simplicity. Your evolution lies in the awareness of your inner child. You are seeing the world for the first time and realizing the wonders around you. Transcend your complications into a simple understanding of this Moment. This is your journey from here to here, transcending into the higher realms of your Being.

Learning must lead to understanding. Apply your knowledge and see where it leads you. Accept the challenge to fly; how else can you test your wings?

We all have come to our present understanding in unusual ways. We were led on specific paths to this point, exactly where we always wanted to be. The key to understanding esoteric scriptures is to realize that God is not an external deity but our Presence. The development of our Soul, the appearance in all its beauty. God is the divinity within you, your ability to Be Present.

I understand now why aspects and symbols of higher worlds sometimes create bafflement and even frustration in me. When I approach the wonders of this world with my intellect, logical thoughts, and doubts, I have lost the child in me.

When I try to find a different answer, dark clouds appear, and my inner light is shadowed. I lose my happiness, curiosity, and wordless presence. My growth is reflected in my ability to be childlike.

"Never imagine wisdom to be more than the under-standing of a child." Rainer Maria Rilke

The Journey Begins

~

"Our friendship is made of being awake." Rumi

Y ou find yourself in a pitch-dark tunnel, struggling to find the exit. But you cannot see anything. So, you bend down and search the rough floor for some matches; a candle might even be found. You crawl around on your hands and knees and finally detect a box of matches. You strike the first match, shining a little light in the dark tunnel. Next, you scan the walls to determine the structure and imagine where the exit might be. Along the way, you strike more and more matches, and your perception and the shape of your prison become more apparent.

Finally, you see a candle, and with much joy, you light the candle. Now you can see the entire length of the tunnel and the door in the far corner.

You walk towards it, and your desperation increases.

The imprisoning tunnel grows more and more frightening. You wonder what you must do to open the door. When you reach it, it is locked. You bang against it, and you cry for help. You shout and hit, and finally, you hear a voice on the other side. It says: "I will help you to open the door, but you need to push against it from the inside. Together we can do it, and you will be free to walk out of this tunnel and into the light."

The tunnel analogy represents the prison we find ourselves in when we question how the world appears. We see our prison in our inability to act and behave differently, not to express negative emotions, or in our shortcomings in loving the people we are close to. First, we start with only a few matches to light our path. With time we find a candle, helping the rest of the way become more precise and accurate. When you arrive at the door to your inner freedom, you need the help of somebody already outside this prison to open the door so you may step out into bliss.

We all need help on our spiritual journey. Without people who have gone this way before us, we cannot succeed.

Thankfully there are many conscious beings we can study and ask for help. They described the way in their writings, paintings, music, and teachings, and by adapting their techniques and guidelines, we can also evolve.

Gautama, the Buddha, said there were many Buddhas before him, and there would be many Buddhas after him.

We can become a Buddha by committing our life to a

specific path, a technique of Awakening. But we do not have to give up our life and move into a Cloister or Ashram. When we have lit the candle, our life provides us the arena for Awakening. Making it out of the tunnel depends on your burning desire to become present. Live your life with love and consideration for others, and it will expand into the growth of your Soul.

Jesus von Nazareth said: *"Many are called, but few are chosen."* My understanding of his words is that many people wish to experience something higher, but only a few try to become the words. Libraries are full of books catering to this fleeting desire.

In addition, almost every newspaper and magazine displays horoscopes and spiritual bits of advice for those who use these ideas as dinner topics or as a part-time hobby.

Why are some people becoming genuine seekers, and others are not? Why can some not fall asleep anymore, cannot go back to a state of mindless activity without the quest to better themselves?

We do not know. There are, though, some theories and concepts that allow some clues.

Astrology might hint at it by proclaiming that a child is born on the exact day, hour, and second when the celestial rays are in mathematical harmony with their individual Karma.

Is this child chosen by *Higher Forces** to follow the path of enlightenment? Are previous lifetimes an indicator of the blueprint, and can this child grasp the Awakening concept?

. . .

I do not know; all theories are speculation. My experiences and incidents led me to this life of searching for a higher truth. I had to become deeply disillusioned with the objects of illusion in life. I had reached the end of my rope when a glimmer of hope appeared on one cold winter day in West Berlin.

Being at a Dead End was my Starting Point.

"Lots of ways to reach God. I chose love." Rumi

Road for Traveling Souls

~

"What stands in the way becomes the way." Marcus
Aurelius

I t would help if you embraced the way by
understanding the way. Observing the way with
simplicity and openness leads you to your Awakening. Knowledge of the outer world limits you. Stones
cannot see; in the beginning, you are like a stone regarding
the divine. Then, when you start to wake up, you learn
to see.

If you know where you want to go, it matters which path
you take.

There are many roads to travel, but only one will lead
you to where you need to be. Along the way, your inner

journey will feed your authentic *Higher Self**. Your true identity is Consciousness itself.

Awakening is a journey, and we find our specific obstacles along the way to encourage evolution. Sure, many elements of this struggle are common for every seeker, but you must discover them yourself.

To get nearer to your Awakening, you must get further away from "I," "me," and "mine."

Your *lower self**, also called ego, or false personality, always tries to find an identity to feel superior to others.

It thrives on the illusion that owning anything will manifest its identification of superiority. The ego equates having with being. I have; therefore, I am. It lives through comparison. The way people see you is the way you perceive yourself.

The collective illusion in society is to equate your possessions with the core of what you are. This belief creates strong prison walls in which your identity is trapped.

The quest to feed on more external things keeps the illusion alive. The need for more leaves us restless and unsatisfied. We become addicts.

To possess is the story of the ego, its need to create identity, to make itself unique.

When you try letting go of your identifications with worldly objects, you will observe that this is an impossible undertaking. The search for a better life, more possessions, and colossal praise is ingrained into the existence of humans.

But you can start to observe these processes in you. As a result, you can shed light on your longings.

You can see the rat race unfolding, but stopping it is impossible. Observe it instead. Stop trying to change things that you cannot change.

Bring light to the automatic processes of the *lower self**. By seeing oneself identified with things, the attachment is not more total. The grip of the ego has been loosened.

Remember, you are not what you observe but what observes; this is the actual transformation. Awareness is the beginning of Spiritual Consciousness.

Some seekers think that renouncing worldly possessions will automatically free them from the identifications of the ego.

Unfortunately, the ego clings to its survival by shifting its identification. Now it will make you believe what an excellent and superior person you have become by giving up your worldly possessions. Some people even enlarge their *lower self** by showing off their outer form of spirituality. Remember, in the beginning, you cannot change anything; you must see, recognize, and observe.

The content of your false personality may change, but its identity remains.

Few people prefer to Be Present in this Moment. Being here and aware is enough for them. This desire is the only way to fulfillment, to happiness. It is who you are, your Consciousness unfolding, coloring your life with joy, harmony, and love.

Those who live a life of love, honesty, and self-sacrifice can awaken.

To do so, we must conquer our negative emotions, the imaginary pictures of ourselves, and the identifications for life's temptations. But within the general direction of our inner work lies a very concrete and specific struggle that is unique in our way.

This struggle concentrates on the two ways of living. One comes from the heart and searches for a connection with the divine. The other caters to the body's desires. We constantly move between these two ways. Try to stay longer on the path of your heart. The rewards are your Presence.

When we enter the way of love, the price and payment are revealed by showing us our main obstacles, the devils of our false personality. Our fate becomes more evident, and we understand that constant effort is required to fulfill our destiny. The main attempt is to Be, to accept the Presence on its term, and to be thankful for life's sufferings.

My personal obstacles to Awakening were resentments of jealousy and envy. It took me many years on my spiritual journey to understand that I was given a specific set of challenges.

Listening to the ever-occurring thoughts in my head, I could detect the broken record of envy and jealousy regarding other people's success, wealth, and luck. These resentments consumed me, and the more I tried to fight them, the more frequently they returned. I prayed and did exercises to gratify the people around me. I would congratulate them on their new car, academic achievement, or house. Still, my heart wasn't really in it. The nagging thoughts appeared again and again.

I transformed the emotions of envy and jealousy when I realized my luck to be connected with Angels and ability to Be Present. In turn, my gratitude grew.

Significant changes have occurred in me that I cannot describe. A sweet fragrance comes from the divine, to waken my senses. The unseen world is more real than the seen. My urge and longing to Be Present grows stronger. I surrender to the miracle of life, to the beauty of my existence. I enjoy the spring in my Soul. The pungent smell of the cleansing lavender, the roses' beauty, and the irises' gentleness emanate in my heart.

When I experience prolonged moments of Awareness, my ability to transform life's friction into acceptance increases, and the thoughts of envy lose their power over me. The more I thank the Gods for finding me worthy of following them, the more the darkness subsides. Finally, I can breathe without being choked by jealousy. What can be more beautiful than one's deliverance, honoring the divine Presence within myself, the miracle of my life?

The precious pearl – one's Soul – can only be produced through the constant transformation of suffering. Therefore, real wealth does not lie in material goods but in the remembrance of one's existence in the Present Moment.

"The profound lesson of reception, nor preference, nor denial." Walt Whitman

The other major obstacle on my road to Awakening was alcohol and its negative effects on inner clarity. As European customs have it, drinking a few glasses of wine at lunch or a shot of Grappa with coffee afterward is acceptable. Unfortunately, this habit became too big for me to handle. So, for a long time, my alcohol intake was too much and it showed in diminished efforts to Be Present.

The realization of my inability to drink wine moderately grew clearer with having to finish any bottle of wine opened. I was unwilling to put it away for tomorrow, to cork it back and forget it. What made it worse was the job I attained while living in London.

After making enough money in Miami Beach, Florida, where I imported Bauhaus and modern classic furniture from Italy, I spent two years in Rome, Florence, and Amsterdam. I wanted to reconnect to the splendors of Europe after years of focusing on making money and enjoying the easy-going life at the beach. But these cities are expensive, and my cash depleted quickly.

Friends in London invited me to visit them and to stay in their beautiful House in North London. I looked for work and strangely accepted an offer from a Speaker Agency in Slough, an hour-long train ride from Paddington Station. My daily commute lasted about two and a half hours, taking the bus, tube, and train before a brisk twenty-minute walk. Today, I can't even fathom what thoughts were running through my mind to say yes to this ordeal. Was it the prospect of money or my idea of writing a book about interviewing the top twenty CEOs in Europe, where I would compile their lessons and advice?

. . .

So, I got up every workday at 4:44 a.m. to be at the agency just before 9 a.m. Suppose you know London and England in general. In that case, you can imagine the weather adding to my ordeal with its oh-so-lovely rain showers, cold gusts of wind, and overall grey skies.

The pressure of a long commute became unbearable, causing "the alcohol escape" – to become more apparent.

After work, I often stopped at the local supermarket to purchase a bottle of wine for the evening to calm me down.

No wonder my writing project fell apart. All the CEOs contacted declined to be part of my project, and the booking of inspirational speakers for company events only showed some meager success.

I quit that job after six months. I was ready and full of hope and vigor to take the best from Europe and transform its beauty inside to create my own beauty. But I was only left with the pieces.

For too long, I had buffered the fact of my slightly greedy nature when it came to bodily pleasures. I did nothing about it till I awoke rudely by my helpless inability not to drink every day.

Now, I have given up alcohol for Spiritual Consciousness. Trading in the stupor of being drunk with the bliss of being alive was a bargain.

No more alcohol for this chap!

But the real lesson in my ordeal was to realize how easy it is to lose the way to Awakening. The poison of alcohol destroyed all my wishes to Be in the Moment; it made me forget my aims and standards.

How easily could the *lower self** have destroyed my Soul? How close did I come to forgetting my aims, to denying my connection with the Gods?

However, my ordeal also made me stronger and clearer not to relinquish my aspirations. I gained Being in the process; I became more focused and destined not to let go of my gift to Awaken.

Every undertaking has intervals among them. First, we are unaware that we are in a gap in our work; we lose the emotional excitement about our efforts by calling them useless; then, we lose faith in our abilities and doubt that something higher even exists.

When we recognize that we are in an interval in our inner work, we already start bridging and overcoming it. You must realize stagnant places within yourself during your journey to your authentic inner Self. Verify the ideas, again and again, that were so precious to you prior. Experience the difference between sleep and Consciousness. Produce the courage to continue. Make little efforts again during your day that help make you more aware.

Take a walk in the park, look at a flower, smell the fragrance, and feel your feet on the ground, the wind touching your face, your hands in your pocket.

Live in the love of Presence. Respond to your inner calling. Do not be distracted by the outside that seeps into you. The outside world is full of agitation. Illusion is a trap.

You do not need any symbols of identity. You are your

own identity by becoming more and more invisible. You have learned that the answer is not words but your inner awareness of this Moment. You are familiar with the divine because some of it is within you. Every sleep ends in waking up. Return; appear.

"To see the Universe itself as a road, as many roads, as roads for traveling souls." Walt Whitman

Conscious Evolution of Mind and Body

∼

"Sistine Chapel – It shows what a Man can do." Johann Wolfgang von Goethe

W hen we start our spiritual journey, we are filled with grand aspirations. Our excitement makes us believe that our nirvana is around the corner and that our strong wish for awakening will sweep away all obstacles and difficulties.

Refrain from seeing your aim to awaken like external aims of making more money, being more successful, or being admired. This longing for your conscious deliverance comes from the wrong place inside you. It is an expression of the *lower self**, your ego, to appear spiritual, to find an identity in the outer form of awakening without grasping the inner meaning. Ambitions need to cease, and wishes need to evaporate into the air so that you are lifted free from the duality of life.

Man's incapacity to see is the veil between the inner and the outer world. A finger shielding your eyes prevents you from seeing the external world. What is hindering you from seeing your inner world is just as small. Find out what it is within you. Only you can know.

Awakening is like practicing a skill, like becoming a good athlete in a particular sport. An athlete understands the daily, extensive training for strength, flexibility, and coordination that will take hours each day to perfect.

Rhythm and timing, response time, and balance are added to the daily routine when you have conquered the more basic skills.

Dedication is the key to continuing our path. Of course, a different technique and approach are necessary, but the actions are the same.

Like some successful athletes who hear the call and have the talent to become outstanding, we, too, hear a buzz. As a result, we become aware of our talent as presence seekers.

We look at a flower and see the enlightenment of the plant reflected in it. We observe a bird and understand that eons ago, it was only an animal crawling along the earth until its transformation brought feathers and flight. Their enlightenment is our mirror.

To achieve excellence in life, we must tackle the laziness of body and mind. As truth seekers, we also must understand that our earthly vessel, our body, needs to be treated well. The ancient saying*' mens sana in corpore sano'* (a sound mind in a healthy body) applies to our efforts to be in the Moment. When we overeat or allow our bodies to deteriorate due to drugs, toxins, or negligence of physical activity, we have no chance to be more awake. Being Present is forming good habits and understanding that allowing your ego free reign destroys your Spiritual Consciousness.

We all have our own story, our own denying forces to create the right environment. For example, William Blake, a British poet and painter in the 18th century whose artistic work reflects his spiritual path, wrote: *"My heart is at rest within my breast, and everything else is still."*

This stillness, this quiet place, needs to be the core of our efforts. The commotions of life, the storms of our outer world, will try to penetrate our inner peace from where our actions stem.

Every human being's story is unique and is the platform for our Awakening. We all experience physical, emotional, and mental pain in our life. But because of this pain, we become a little stronger and wiser. Growing through this pain, we acquire greater compassion and perspective.

Remember, every fairytale is based upon the transformation of suffering. So, you would like to win the prince or overcome the evil witch. In that case, you must go through ordeals, give up your identification and become forgiving and heartfelt.

At the same time, we do not have to pretend to like difficulties when encountering them, but we can understand their value and place in our journey. We need to keep the thread of attention that they are hidden gifts. How we respond to them, and the ability to embrace or push them away will also decide how often we must face them repeatedly. They are like school lessons, where one can move on only to the next chapter when the previous task is learned and understood.

Suffering opens the heart, and that is a beautiful aspect. Pain and difficulties are spring thunderstorms, dark clouds above, and rejuvenation below. The human world is the home where the body hurts and the Soul rejoices. In our world, thorns and poisonous plants grow wild, but roses and vegetables need the care of a gardener.

What would be a practical approach to catalyzing change? First, we need to be realistic with ourselves. When things are going great, we want it to stay that way. We cherish our current life when life is good. But it doesn't always happen that way. Change is part of life, especially when faced with trouble and difficulties. And once a problem does arise, we hope for change and embrace it willingly, hoping it will stop the pain. But then, once things have become "normal and acceptable" again, we hold tight to the status quo and are afraid of change again.

For some people, even slight disturbances cause them distress and suffering. Therefore, part of Awakening is also to keep these problematic endeavors in perspective and not to enlarge them with our identification and self-pity.

. . .

There are two kinds of changes: external and internal changes. I came from a place focused on external changes, improving the world around me by changing systems and other people. In its simplest form, political activism changes the injustices in life by pointing the finger outward while disregarding how the other four fingers simultaneously point toward oneself. Revolting and openly expressing dissatisfaction with political situations or actors gives the *lower self** energy and sustains their existence.

What I decide to focus on expands. If I give love, then love can grow.

What matters are the internal changes that allow me to help make a difference in my life? Observe the nature of your being in the different ways you act, respond, and live. This is who you are, your Essence.

For some people, there is a contradiction between internal and external change. They direct their attention outward and do not understand that what they condemn also manifests within them. How can there be peace when I cannot stop expressing my negative emotions? Why am I incapable of forgiving somebody for little, unimportant acts?

A step towards internal change means doing things for something other than grand purposes. Otherwise, you set up imaginary pictures on a screen, keeping you from seeing the actual landscape.

Only the work on oneself can give the clarity and the courage to address injustice in this world. Only when I know who I am in this world can I exert the proper leverage at the right place and time to make a difference in this world?

Both changes do not exclude each other; the outer change cannot occur without the inner and vice versa.

"For a day, just for one day, talk about that which disturbs no one and brings peace into your beautiful eyes." Hafiz

Acceptance

~

"The most important hour is always the present. The most important person is the one sitting right from you. The most necessary work is always Love." Meister Eckhart

Acceptance leads to gratitude. Our fate depends on our past. Our past lifetimes are the measures of our existence today. Maybe because you struggled with your childhood, you have cursed your parents, but those struggles were given to you to understand and awaken. You become closer to your fate when you let go of all your expectations of how life should unfold.

The Story of the Wise Man

. . .

There was an old farmer who was well respected by those who knew him. Then, one day the farmer's horse ran away. Upon hearing the news, his neighbors came to visit. "Such bad luck," they said sympathetically.

"Maybe," the farmer replied.

The following day, the horse returned, bringing three other wild horses with it. "How wonderful!" the neighbors exclaimed.

"Maybe," replied the old man.

The following day, his son tried to ride one of the untamed horses, was thrown, and broke his leg. The neighbors expressed their sympathy for this misfortune. '

"Maybe," answered the farmer.

The day after, military officials came to the village to draft young men into the army. But, seeing that the son's leg was broken, they passed him by. The neighbors congratulated the farmer on how well things had turned out.

"Maybe," said the farmer.

Do not judge anything that comes your way. Instead, see it as necessary for your evolution. Everything has a meaning, something you cannot see yet but only sense. Do not mind what happens.

When you resist what happens to you, you are under the power of the *lower self**. Negative emotions are poison to our bodies. It leads to unhappiness, which can create despair. The ego thrives on misery. It needs to feed on negativity, anger, fear, and resentment.

Positive emotions have a positive effect on our bodies. People, though, do not understand that the so-called positive emotions generated from our ego already carry the negativity within. For example, anticipation turns into disappointment; praise turns into criticism. These positive emotions have the opposite in them. Only positive emotions generated within your *Higher Self** do not bring the opposite.

Unfortunately, the mind carries negative emotions within it. It does not let go. We add a burden on top of the load with our memories. This creates our story, our baggage. But the past cannot prevent you from being present now.

When you start to be fed up with your negativity and identification, you begin the journey toward Awakening. The suffering you experience is necessary on this journey—it will allow you to see yourself. To see, to know that you are in the prison of your false personality, is an essential realization. Do not despair; it is good. The light in your inner darkness has been illuminated.

Cease seeing yourself as a victim. Nobody does anything to you. You allow those things to happen to you. Do not be your little false personality, complaining about people, bad luck, health, or the weather. Change it with the realization of your abundance, your inner richness, and your understanding. Give, and it will be given to you. This is part of knowing yourself, the most significant revelation of discovering who you are.

"To the one who has more will be given, and from the one who has not, even what he has will be taken away." Jesus Christ

. . .

Know yourself instead of knowing about yourself. First, you need to learn to study yourself correctly. It is not about knowledge but about Being. Be yourself; step away from the information about you and become yourself. Just Be Now Here.

The mind carries negative emotions within it. It does not let go. It holds it within itself for years and even decades. Do not add a burden on top of a burden with your memories. This creates our attachments and our sleep.

The past cannot prevent you from being present now.

Find your higher order. Align with your purpose. See the order beyond the chaos. To do so, be quiet inside and look beyond your thinking. Refrain from explaining. Instead, understand harmony by being conscious of it. This will allow you to step out of the maze of good or bad.

Realize that this moment is your life. Make it your friend, do not resist it. Embrace it, no matter what it holds.

When you are Present, there is no time. Time only exists in your memory or in your anticipation. This moment happens now; your life unfolds. Do you understand the gift given to you?

It is impossible to resist this gift, to go against it. Typically, a difficult destiny will arise in people looking for specific reactions, which will only prolong the same fate in future lives. The only way to make our destiny unique is to accept it, not rebel against it.

Turn the unfavorable elements of your fate, like losing loved ones, enduring a physical illness, or emotional distress, into advantages. When you accept your destiny, you turn the blows of chance into a supernatural power that will lift you into your own Awakening. Do not make a demand on the world but make an even greater demand on yourself.

It is also crucial that all open accounts need to be balanced in life and beyond, and all unfinished business needs to be resolved. The wise woman will pay off her debts before they become due. The understanding that certain payments are required in life brings one to the point of accepting anything that comes one's way. We must view our life regarding our many lifetimes without complaining about the universe asking us to pay another installment.

We become free by accepting cause and effect in our lives. Therefore, do not resist the forces working upon you. We do not see the future; therefore, we cannot imagine that a specific struggle or misfortune is a blessing.

All circumstances will change in time. For example, people believe they will never be happy after a tragic accident or a devastating loss. However, empirical psychology has proven that after six months, the lottery winner is as happy or unhappy as they were before. The same result also applies to paraplegic people who, after six months, are similarly happy or sad as they were before their tragic accident.

. . .

People are full of contradictions. Why can we not accept them? Why can't we swallow down our judgment and see it for what it is? And what it is precisely: Nothingness.

Understand it is nothingness, and then we will see our inconsistencies and shortcomings. This is Awakening. To observe, separate, and accept. Stay focused on your Consciousness. Life is full of difficulties and problems. Be different. See them as stepping stones for your Awakening. Did you believe Awakening would be a walk in the park? Are the sufferings of Jesus Christ on the cross not necessary? Accept your sufferings, embrace them, and hold them dear. Only then is awakening possible. Be strong.

How many witches were burned on the stake, and how many martyrs were crucified? Be like Paul, who refused to be crucified like Christ and requested to hang upside down. Embrace your suffering; it only makes you a God. Do not complain and find rescue from someone pitying you. Only the strong evolve. Be strong now. Paradise is near; stepping into it means letting go of your resentments, fear, and concerns. We need to remove our old attitudes and simply accept who we are. Devote yourself to a worthy cause. What can be more beautiful than being present in one's life? Consciousness is not function. One day this body will perish. The Soul continues.

"There is no miracle but seeing your own beloved." Rumi

Do Something Right Now

≈

"Presence is profound because it is simple." Robert Burton

Observing is Doing.
See the negative thoughts of the *lower self**
as what they are: human-waste products of the
mind.

One needs to recognize the basic mechanics of the ego,
identifying the dealings of this imposter that believes in its
superiority.

Awakening happens in acknowledging the culprit and
understanding its lies. Then, your Consciousness starts to
flower. We must strengthen it by observing and dissecting
these dark processes that keep us asleep.

. . .

You cannot fight against the dark forces, but you can observe them and slowly loosen their grip on you.

Something fundamental must change within you to recognize this if you wish for sanity. This paradigm shift is a gift bestowed on you through experiences in different lifetimes.

Your insanity ends when sanity appears, the beginning of seeing your inner, mechanical unconscious working.

The truth is not your thought but the awareness outside of thought. Consciousness exists outside of the mind and body. Outside of the learned identity, the "I," "Me," and "Mine." Let go of such forms, belief systems, and identifications.

But you can let go by not naming things in your life. Instead, see the reality behind the label, and experience the connection beyond the words and thoughts. Can a word explain who you are? Can your Being be described with words?

Understand the illusion in your life, the stories they told you since birth, the ones of being somebody or nobody, the ones achieving richness or staying poor. You take the first step toward Awakening when you understand these illusions are not real.

Whenever you say "I," you have lost the connectedness to yourself. The sense of self, the rise of identity as me and mine, gives you a false sense of who you are. But this is not you, just your limited ego.

Shift your identity from the content of your voice inside you to the awareness of this voice. Allow for real inner change and work on it so it may happen now.

Read this sentence while feeling the book in your hand. See the whole page and not only the separate line. Observe your breath, hear the sound around you, and notice the light. It will take us this Moment, this minute, our whole lifetime, to live the question of what is real change.

Rainer Maria Rilke, the German Conscious Poet, said it bluntly:

"Live the question; eventually, you will grow into the answer."

What control do we have? Do we control the thoughts that arise in our minds or our reactions to these thoughts?

Even if we read all the books on positive thinking and mental attitudes, we would still not achieve the goal of procuring only positive thoughts. This promise is an illusion. We do not have a spam filter in our heads; much of that unfiltered junk still reaches us.

We only have the power to not respond to the negative thoughts in our minds and not believe them. Doing so gives us great strength and is the only refuge from this world. One must find peace inside oneself to accept this. Do not worry about negative thoughts, do not give them space and energy. Think about something positive or someone you are thankful for. Look around you and see the beauty. We all have thoughts of sorrow, fear, and resentment. It is within our ability not to invite these thoughts for tea but to let them go, watch them as if they were a fleeting black cloud that will soon disappear when our sun of love and happiness shines through.

Our emotions are almost impossible to control. We feel instantly, and managing emotions once they've appeared is impossible. They are too fast for our intellectual perception and are already there before we can detect and control them. In the Chapter "Four Brains," you will hear about the much higher speed of the Emotional Brain and the inability of our Intellectual Brain to control them.

We must find a different technique to help battle negative emotions. Gautama, the Buddha, discovered breath as the best indicator of rapid change in our emotional world. He found that our breath changes when intense emotions start to appear. Observing one's breath and seeing the changes occurring in moments of intense emotions is a step to separate our *Higher Self** from the external storms battering our calm inner waters.

When we observe ourselves, we notice that a rush of negative emotions has been boiling up in us for some time. Then we release them through an incident like lava from an erupting volcano. There is no justification for allowing negative emotions to destroy our inner peace and harmony. Negative emotions negate Presence. Negative emotions are the poison we drink, assuming it will hurt the other person.

· · ·

Spiritual life is a life where we try not to react and get shaken so often we are no longer shakable. Let go of your immediate reactions, access the power of non-reaction, the ability to be free of the entanglement to this world of illusions.

It isn't easy to see the truth about oneself. Be small, be humble, and do not show off with false values. Be still inside. Do not name or explain the things outside of yourself. They happen as it rains or snows. This realization is the beginning of our journey.

The major challenge in our life remains: allowing beneficial influences entering our life. Consider our knowledge that regular, positive mental exercises are good for us. But although we know this, most of us do not do it.

Let's imagine you wake up, and before getting out of bed, you say: "I am happy to be alive." After one month of saying this sentence daily, you can add a minute of positive reflection as you start the day.

Although you might find this childish, it is essential and translates into your daily efforts To Be Here Now. First, it shows you were committed to your aim. You set aside some time every day for your positive mind routine. And most of all, a little of something is better than much of nothing.

Being present in one Moment in your life is the beginning. Take on only a little. Unfortunately, we tend to aim too high and load ourselves with tasks and exercises only to prove that we can only do some of them. We then call ourselves a loser and destroy our joy and happiness with negative feelings and thoughts. This form of self-destruction comes from our *lower self**, an evil force in us that bombards our quest for a fulfilling life with self-doubt and negativity.

When you start with something simple, like Being Present in one Moment of your life, you will get the taste of Being Present in more Moments.

It is excellent and beneficial to dream big but start small and connect the dots as you go. As the Chinese philosopher Lao Tzu said, *"Every Journey begins with the first step."*

Our efforts to live a spiritual life can seem overwhelming. But only the student is complicated; the lesson is easy.

Focus on the simple things in life, the daily routines where you introduce a new little concept. It is a miracle to add Presence to the daily routines we do. Brushing your teeth and feeling the handle of your toothbrush in your hand, zipping up a zipper intentionally, sensing the car door handle while opening the door. We are repeating the same routines every day. Our chance for Awakening is to experience these small, unspectacular events as the core of our life. Allow yourself to be pulled towards Consciousness.

When you feel overwhelmed by the challenges in your life and the many things you must do, take them from moment to moment—one thing at a time. Open your eyes when you wake up, lift away your bed cover, sit up, and place your feet on the ground. Stand up and be thankful for a new day to arise, one more chance to be alive.

Our life unfolds in small increments—one step at a time. Be present and aware of each Moment, and do not hurry beyond the Presence. Life becomes real when you realize you can only simultaneously do, think, or feel one thing at a time. Make it a joyous experience.

We are only able to have one thought at a time. So, choose a positive one and turn away from the negative one. We are only able to do one thing right at a time. Focus on that one thing and forget the modern lie about multitasking. We can only feel one emotion at a time. Make it beautiful, something to cherish.

There's a simple concept: Here and Now – Breathing in and out - focusing - coming back to the Moment is all we need to walk on our spiritual path. We are remembering where we are, conceiving this Moment, and not anticipating what might happen next.

Mark Twain said:

> *"I had many troubles in my life, most of which never happened."*

Our fears are self-created and imaginary concepts about what might happen in the future. Unhappiness is a disease. Negativity is polluting our existence. Regrets, anxieties, the past, and the future are mind concepts created by your ego.

But this Moment is different; you can enjoy the beauty of Being Present. Use this Moment to be present and walk further toward liberation and bliss. It is simple, and therefore our ego makes it complicated. The quality of this Moment reflects the quality of our life.

Allow your Consciousness to expand inside you.

"The state will be perfected and become a waking reality, which a little while ago we attempted to create as a dream and an idea only." Plato, The Laws

Aspects of Inner Work

~

"Man will not exert efforts for what he imagines possessing already." Epictetus

The sophistication of your excuse is not considered.

Results take work, but the effort is simple. Unfortunately, your imaginary efforts cannot lead to anything. Just be Here Now. No pretense or showing off. Feel your feet on the ground, the weight of this book you hold, and the light shining through the window. This is Awakening, a simple effort to be in this Moment, whatever it brings. It might not be grand, it might not be something to talk about, but it is your Presence, simple and pure.

Did you imagine your Awakening would be announced with trumpets and festivities? Realize that you are going against life's chains meant to hold you down. Remember that you are special to have recognized the prison you and your fellow humans are caught in. Be thankful that you understand and have awakened from the dream of non-existence.

We falsely believe that only great efforts – like trekking in the Himalayas or fasting for weeks- dramatically change our lives. Therefore, we miss the moment-by-moment opportunity to make small but real-life changes.

Now is the Moment. Do you hear the sounds around you? Do you sense your breath? Do you see your hands, the space you are in? Simplicity is the ultimate sophistication; realize it. This Moment contains miracles.

Early in my inner work, I succumbed to the general frenzy and went to see Harrison Ford in "The Blade Runner."

Many of the surreal scenes remained vivid in my memory. My inner work had made me more receptive, and my openness has made me vulnerable. I could not let go of these images after seeing the movie.

I remember leaving the movie theater in a heightened state of awareness. I was pumped with energy, and my emotional state was disturbed. The dramatic elements swirled in my body, encouraging me to just start walking and walking. It was a cold October evening, and I walked straight to the Berlin Wall. Having reached it, I just moved along next to it, seeing the same surreal pictures I had experienced in the movie. It gave me some relief. The cold wind cleared my mind, and the fast pace of my walk slowly burned off the extra energy.

Although this experience is carved in my memory (and is memory not what we want to achieve?), it has become clear that I do not wish to have these impressions in my life.

In every moment, we add new experiences to our existence. The quality and substance of these impressions are crucial for our aim to awaken.

We choose what kind of input we invite into our life. We have the responsibility for our Awakening to choose wisely.

If we are serious about our inner work, we need to select something that promotes our growth, something we want to make part of our life. Make it a flower instead of trash, a symphony instead of noise, and a painting instead of darkness. Do not allow the ego to tarnish your mind with negative impressions.

Our mind will always be an extension of our ego, our false personality. It races from topic to topic without rhyme or reason, pure insanity. The only difference between the so-called "normal people" and "crazy people" is that this rat race occurs in our heads. "Sane" people typically do not formulate this craziness in public, but occasionally I can hear myself talking out loud in privacy.

It is our mind that binds us, and it is also the mind that can set us free. Our mind tells us about all our responsibilities, tasks, and duties. You do not need to listen to it; you are free from all worldly boundaries when you reach the spirit of your Awakening.

You can understand these words but still need time to experience them. It starts with not listening anymore to your false personality.

The ego also causes people to not feel who they are, forcing them to fill their life with possessions that give them a sense of identity. Instead, seek solitude within your own Self, do not renounce the world, but choose wisely which world you like to invite into your life.

Love yourself, and you will be able to love the world. The more Present you become, the more your valuation of the simple moments increases. Finally, your gratitude becomes real.

Life gives you the experiences you need when you are on the way to Awakening. You might not be aware of the lessons in the beginning, but with time, you will first see and then understand them. Sometimes it might take years to recognize these lessons, and your resistance to them fades slowly. When you start to let go, your Being gets more robust and your mind weaker. You will recognize these experiences as a gift: the reminder of a different world, the emergence of your *Higher Self**.

If you calmly perform the required tasks and don't allow yourself to be distracted but focus on keeping your spirit pure, you will live a happy life. Be confident and truthful;

observe yourself as a stranger but love yourself as you love your beloved. No one can destroy your spirit, and no one can harm your Awakening.

One cannot learn to awaken. It must be experienced.

Start by letting go of your mind and the myriad of considerations. Take responsibility for who you are. Find yourself. Do not follow the herd mentality. Be not afraid of the unknown. It is the only place worth exploring. Shine your light into this place and embrace the challenge. You can only grow spiritually.

Remember, the past and future do not exist. They are just thought concepts, living only in our mind. Give up the need to impress other people. Cease seeing yourself as a victim. Challenge your own demons. Emerge as who you are meant to be. How much are you willing to pay for this gift? It is cheap; you give up nothing for everything. Your imaginary picture does not exist; your responsibilities are just mental constructs; your regrets and anticipations are just illusions— exchange nothing for the gift of Awakening.

Make your life meaningful with the understanding that nothing matters besides Being Present in this Moment. Love your life, no matter what is in it. Imagine living this same life over and over in endless recurrence. Are your values worth reliving? Are you proud and happy with what you are doing? Break the chains of your prison.

"We are always on the same internal journey, no matter where we are." Robert Burton

Developing Talent for Awakening

~

"Fairy Tales do come true for us." Robert Burton

Simplicity opposes hypocrisy with a beautiful sincerity and a hint of vulnerability. Simplicity wants to do the work without shining in the light of praise, without recognition and advantage. To Be Here is enough.

Two Conscious Beings told us about their Spiritual Consciouness:

> *"Everything comes down to one thing – staying awake." Buddha*

> *"Remain here and stay awake with me." Jesus Christ*

. . .

How do we develop our talent for Awakening further? Many of you – like myself – have traveled the world, read books, heard lectures and seminars, and met teachers and wise men. However, you must realize that the preparation is over. You are made ready enough to tackle the inner fight and embrace your moments in life. There is no alternative, no more excuses or illusions of other riches.

The Story how Rumi Met Shams

"Jalaluddin Rumi is sitting by a fountain in Konya, talking to students. His father Bahauddin's notebook, the Maarif, is open on the fountain ledge. Shams interrupts and pushes the precious text into the water. 'Why are you doing this?' asks Rumi, protesting that this is the only copy of Bahauddin's precious thoughts. 'It is time to live what you have read and talked about. But if you want, I can retrieve the book. It will be perfectly dry. See?' He lifts Bahauddin's book out, dry."

Your path has led you to live and learn The Art of Being Here Now. You understand that this Art has become the ultimate quest in your life.

Remember, everyone is the most important person you will ever meet. At least everyone thinks this way about themselves. Human beings are self-centered. Everything evolves around "I." We all have vanity as the main feature of our existence. This vanity feature becomes so obsessive for some people that their behavior becomes ridiculous in many ways. To wake up and be present in one's life demands taking oneself less seriously. I do not mean one's outer appearance or choosing the best things in life that one can afford, but rather to realize that this body, this existence, will soon disappear. Death comes swiftly, and even an entire life of eighty-plus years vanishes fast. Gratitude and Thankfulness are the antipodes of vanity.

To walk the path of Awakening, one must find this quiet place inside where worldly thoughts of importance and superiority cannot reach.

George Gurdjieff, the Conscious Being promoting the "Fourth Way" as a method for Awakening, said: *"Think and do the opposite of what normal life does and you will be closer to the truth."*

Life copies life, and conformity in behavior and action is a trap for human beings. Trends and fashion are based on this concept. Add some slogans of individuality and choice, and you have the uniqueness of millions of people wearing ripped jeans.

Awakening is part of a definite paradigm shift in our thoughts and emotions. Therefore, the question must always be, "Does this help my evolution, or does this hinder my aim?"

Our new life needs clear markers that we set for ourselves. These are the standards we introduce into our life. Make them small and unpretentious, so you cannot brag to others about these simple things. For you, these are invisible reminders of your inner efforts to stay present in your life.

You will find them for yourself by looking at the most mechanical aspects of your life. Pay attention to the daily activities where you are mostly asleep, the thoughts and emotions ingrained into you by copying other people and being taught that this is the way to do them.

To help myself, I use different wake-up calls. Changing them regularly is necessary because our *lower self** knows quickly how to make these intentionally introduced habits similar to any other mechanical action.

To stay Awakened, there are some things I do and have done to be more intentional: Making my bed with a focus on details like one would notice done at a fine hotel. Hanging up my clothes instead of throwing them over a chair. Reading a poem or uplifting story in the morning instead of the newspaper. Driving at the speed limit to work. Not eating while standing and setting down my knife and fork after every bite. Looking people in the eyes while greeting them, and not using my hands to gesture while speaking.

We have a large toolbox to use to break the momentum of our mechanical life. Yes, these efforts interrupt your smooth sailing through life. Their task is to function as stumbling block, interrupting your activities and bringing you back to the Moment.

This Moment is always available to us. Give your Conscious Self a push to Presence with clear thinking.

When you master yourself, you are free. Free of judgment, free of negativity. Rise above imagination to the Presence of your Soul. You must be in a place beyond words—where words cannot reach you. Transcend the ordinary into the sublime. Attach your world to the Gods.

And keep it simple. Leonardo da Vinci noted that *"simplicity is the ultimate sophistication."*

Unfortunately, our *lower self** tries to make things complicated.

But now, the only spiritual life you need is not to react. Perception without process brings enlightenment. Your Soul sees things as they are, so create a space between an event and your reaction. Remember your breath. Remember your aim. Remember that friction is done for you to jolt you into Presence. The difficulties you are going through are not directed against you; they are produced for you.

Be clever, be present in a world that is primarily asleep and unaware that it is sleeping. Keep the essential questions of life within your grasp. *"To Be or not To Be" and "What is truth?"* are everlasting questions for us to answer in our own words. Therefore, be definite in your purpose.

It helps to identify oneself with a successful image. Find a person you admire, have a picture of them in your home, and ask yourself what this person would do in various situations you are confronted with.

Find a slogan or quote you love and read it aloud daily

to guide you. Break the pattern of defeat; become the hero in your life.

You are brilliant in many ways. Even if you are appointed in life to minor tasks, realize that the distinction of a man is not brought to him by what he does. Still, always bring excellence to everything you do. Anything you do well is noble, no matter how humble or minor.

It is not a palace or a position that makes someone unique, but royal behavior does. The perfection of character, to live your days as if they could be your last days, without frenzy or pretense, putting a fine polish on all the things you do, is a life worth living.

Excellence is not reserved for special situations. How you handle yourself, the attitudes you express throughout life, and the importance you see in anything that comes your way will make a difference in your ability to Be Present. To Be in the Moment, you must first be aware and attentive. This is the beginning of your ability to Be Conscious in your life.

Your efforts to Be Here Now are not something you occasionally do. It is not reserved for the quiet moments when you are alone and everything seems okay. To Be Present in your life is something you do every second. It does not matter what you do; you bring Presence to everything. Your profound focus on the Presence is all that matters. Do not let people tell you otherwise. Refrain from disturbing your efforts to grasp the Moment. You are given the power to choose reality; who would choose imagination instead? Use your time to Awaken.

This is your life, do not be afraid to live it by your aspirations and your quest for excellence. It all passes by quickly. Grab it before it slips through like the sand in an hourglass.

"In the faces of men and women, I see God and my face in the Glass." Walt Whitman

Every Moment Counts

~

"There is no tomorrow, only a series of Nows." Robert Burton

The Art of Being Here Now is the Art of focusing on this Moment in your life. You are reading this sentence, and it should stop you in your track. Right now, there is an opportunity to Be Present. Now you can be aware of your feet, mindful of the noises around you, and aware of your breath.

Every Moment is precious. There is no ranking of worthwhile moments to experience and others to forget. Even the moments on the toilet or the moments of embarrassment are yours and are part of your life. The simplicity of holding a glass of water, lifting it to one's mouth, and taking a sip is a miracle once you see and experience it.

Our ability to awaken depends upon Being Present everywhere and at every time. Therefore, cherish all Moments in your life and do not mentally divide them into good or bad, worthy or unimportant. It is your life, comprised of 86,400 seconds per day.

Nothing exists beyond this present Moment. They become unattainable to us when they have passed, leaving behind only a memory of something that has happened.

Our future only exists in our imagination. It might be fearful anticipation of what the future might bring or the lively imagination of something good or beautiful happening to us. As we probably already learned, this thinking is untrue and often unfounded. Most of our fears live only in the future. If you start imagining the future as beautiful, it will turn into joy and happiness. But if you continue to suspect it to be dreadful and full of sorrow, it will turn into the nightmare your mind created it to be so.

To Be Here Right Now is the only jewel we genuinely possess. This Moment can be beautiful or challenging; it can find us in despair, joy, agony, or ecstasy, but it is the only one we can perceive. We can make this Moment ours forever.

Our only destination in life is Presence.

Robert Burton says: *"The Present might not be beautiful, but it is always beautiful to be Present."*

Everything happens only in this Moment. Only now my life exists. One does not exist in the past or future. The only place where you can find yourself is in the Presence. There is nothing more exciting than Being Present in one's own life.

Today is an excellent opportunity to begin, no matter your age. Looking back in a few years, today will seem like when you were young and full of potential. You will think of how you could have started something new or made a decision that may have benefitted your future. So, save your time. Could you do it now?

We need to realize that we constantly think about the past or future. To Be in the Moment is quite unsettling for many people. Therefore, people immediately take out a telephone or another device to distract themselves when they must stop moving, all because they fear experiencing the Moment. Everything else becomes more important than just looking around, realizing where one is, and regarding one's environment. But it would be best to find the courage to experience it.

For example, you enter a doctor's office. You sit down, look at the other people waiting, smile, and take in the impressions of the room. You sense your body on the chair, your feet on the ground, and just be content to have arrived.

This attention requires effort. To be drifted away is effortless.

We are constantly confronted with mind wandering.

Yet, staying focused on one topic or mental aim is only possible with training to teach oneself to become quiet inside.

Try this experiment:

Start a timer and try not to have any thoughts for one minute. You will notice that all kinds of thoughts will rush into your head - thoughts unrelated to this Moment, unrelated to each other, a wild rollercoaster in your mind.

Are you aware that when you sit down to listen to a concert, your mind is suddenly rushing around, experiencing thoughts interfering with your ability to enjoy the music effectively? An explanation of this disturbing element in our inability to concentrate is found in the Chapter "Our Four Brains." The Moving Brain instigates this useless mind activity, which will barrage us with thoughts when we stop moving.

This wild ride in our heads becomes even more apparent when we meditate. For example, trying to sit and observe our breath is an almost impossible task. Being aware of the breath coming in and going out, we constantly drift away. We are talking to ourselves about an unpleasant encounter with a stranger last night or thinking about the breakfast to prepare afterward. Meditating shows us the truth about ourselves: our mind is wandering. A wild animal jumps without rhyme or reason to unrelated events, feelings, and thoughts. Observing this during quiet moments of meditation opens our understanding of the obstacles in our spiritual journey ahead.

But this hyper brain activity is constantly happening; we always wander in our minds to engage with our preferred thoughts, worries, fears, or identifications. This inner voice never stops. We are so used to it that we can only hear it in our moments of stillness.

We all have our preferred topics when we interact with this inner voice. We have thoughts almost every second of our waking life; they tend to be mostly old ones, recycled repeatedly.

New thoughts are seldom and happen primarily in unfamiliar circumstances when we are on vacation or doing something out of the ordinary. Otherwise, we are kept in our thought-prison day in and day out.

Observing what kind of thoughts are most prominent in you is crucial. I have seen that mine are primarily negative ones following a distinct thought pattern. They tend to be about injustice, jealousy, envy, and judgment.

These inner talks revolve around the unfair behaviors of others towards me, how they treated me wrongly, and how great I responded to these challenges. Our thoughts are an inner race between good or bad, like or dislike, beautiful or ugly. By being asleep, we do not notice them. We are used to it; we think it is normal.

We are not what we observe. We are the observer.

. . .

Understanding this concept is our liberation, our path to freedom from our mechanical life. The human body and the brain have all kinds of useless expressions that we are typically not aware of. The voice in our head is the voice of the *lower self**, judging the world, other people, and ourselves—a waste of time.

The ego allows for the endless tapes that are rewinding themselves while shaving, showering, or eating. I am tired of these harmful, ever-recurring thoughts. These dark modes of despair and hate, the quivers of our suffering, need to be replaced with wishes of well-being for others, with thanks for their kindness, love, and the beauty of our life.

So I read the beautiful reflections of philosophers, poetry, and inspirational messages, but still, the resentful thoughts do not stop. Why can I not get away from all these negative thoughts? Why not replace them with positive ones that speak of the beauty of being alive, watching a sunset at the beach or a sunrise on my porch?

Because this is the *lower self's** ammunition, *it* will not stop interfering with our evolution. It will always try to find a weak spot in our efforts to love, in our work to Be Present. But the ego is getting weaker. Specific negative processes in our brains can only work in the darkness. When we shine a light, see the reality of our existence, and look into the sunshine of our life, we become immune to its poison.

We must only observe and understand that we are not what we observe. Our Soul is separate from the bickering and fighting of the mechanical world. It exists on an entirely different mental plane.

. . .

My experience of a *Higher State** driving on the German Autobahn made me understand:

I was driving back home from a weekend visit with friends. It was a late Sunday afternoon on a sunny August day. Reminiscing about the beautiful encounter I had just spent with my friends and our lively conversations, I was cruising along. All of a sudden, my perception changed. The dark asphalt and the white lines dividing the lanes on the Autobahn became more prominent. I saw my hands holding the steering wheel, but my eyes didn't see this. Something was looking through my eyes: my Soul appeared. I kept driving. I saw the world around me, the cars passing, the trees along the road, the grass, and the crash barrier. Everything was good and was part of this world.

My Awakening lasted for almost thirty minutes. I was driving my car as usual, and then Spiritual Consciousness appeared. There were no thoughts about the past or future. I was just Being Present without mechanical behavior interfering. Eventually, my mind began to worry about how long I could sustain this Spiritual Consciousness. The Moment I marveled at my experience, I fell back into my ordinary consciousness.

This long period of being alive showed me that my Higher Self* is separate from my body, thoughts, sensations, and feelings. It appears independent from the human form. It was looking through my eyes and arising independently.

The *Higher Self**, my Soul, can exist without the body; it will continue after my physical death. It exists forever.

To let our Soul appear, we need to create a space. This space lies between stimulus and response. In this Moment of stillness and non-reaction lies our freedom and power to choose our answer. Our response carries growth and independence.

I have started to see this. I am tired of these thoughts and opinions about how life should be and how life needs to unfold to make me happy. I have given up the fundamental ideas of how I must be, think and act. Now, those little moments while I am Present are the moments I choose to be thankful for. For example, seeing a Hummingbird drinking from the provided feeder makes me happy, and a flower growing on an old rosebush brings me joy. These experiences are my happiness level, and I accept them willingly and thankfully.

"The lower self creates the illusion that simple moments are not important enough." Robert Burton

Love - Nothing but Love

~

"The aim of Love is the everlasting possession of the Good."
Diotima (Socrates's Teacher)

Every seeker of Spiritual Consciousness is taking her initiation with love. Love is a cosmic power that reveals to man the world of understanding, the realm of miracles.

Love is selfless and free of fear. It pours itself out without demanding any return. Love's joy is in giving without asking for any return.

Love is the most vital force in the universe. Tap into this force by giving up your expectations and requests; you are becoming the love that conquers sleep. Love does not seek or demand but draws its likeness within this world.

. . .

Not having achieved eternal bliss, we do not yet have the concept of "real love," but our efforts of Being Present give us a glimpse into this beautiful existence

Without love, spirituality cannot be achieved. Without love, you are just a dull vessel without sound or meaning. Everything starts and ends with this kind of love that does not demand or request; it is plentiful.

Therefore, we need to work on achieving this love. Ask to be freed from resentment, hate, jealousy, or judgment. Look at yourself and count the endless moments during your day when you have forgotten this simple message. So many little incidents hold us captive, and so many minor events become the mountains of our negativity. So much is lost within our imagination of being right and judging others wrong.

We are ordinarily tyrannical and selfish in our affection. We give love as a gift when our needs are met, and only then do we deem the receiver worthy of our love.

Our jealousy is the worst enemy in our quest for real love. We are jealous of somebody more successful, luckier, more anything. See your pattern; despise these habits and understand that nothing meaningful can ever be achieved unless you give a little of this true love. Try to salute the divinity in other people; see them as part of God's creation.

It is so easy to love a woman or a man you fall in love with. No efforts were involved; nothing special concerning your Awakening.

Love somebody who despises you, somebody who harms you, and the kingdom of Heaven will be bestowed upon you. Yes, this is difficult; this is almost impossible, but you want to become a Conscious Being. Don't you? This is the price to pay. Give up your self-righteousness, your knowledge; you're judging. Observe yourself in these dark moments and realize that you are not better but luckier by seeing these patterns.

Love is to Be Present in our life. If one is awake, one can love; if one is asleep, one cannot. Love is giving attention to people and the things around us. Love is spreading our energy, our God-like appearance. It is the gift we share in this world and one we shall reclaim in the manifold.

True hearts are looking for love constantly. So, hold gold in your heart, do not allow anybody to turn it into mud.

Love happens in the Present, at this Moment. Love reflects the God-like attitude to the world and affects everything and everybody in it. When I am in love, the world is beautiful. I smile at the world, and it shines back at me.

Being in love is Being Present. Being Present is to understand that only love can conquer sleep.

I remember being in love the first time. Such love is given to us because we are once mechanically allowed to see our Soul, our destination, and our ability to be like a God.

I was Hercules when I met her; I could do anything for her. I saw only stars and flowers. She was the most beautiful woman I had ever seen. Her words, smile, and movements were like a goddess speaking to me. I saw nothing besides her; I would have freely given my life if she had asked. I was her slave, her servant, her protector. I was in love, and anybody who understands these words is fortunate to have been given this glimpse into eternity.

I am not talking about these experiences of being in love as a substitute for Awakening, but it is as close as we ever come to Being Present and alive before connecting with our Higher Self*. This love was a gift from the Gods, a peak into what is possible. Now is the time to do it intentionally, allowing this love to appear.

Imagine creating these emotions and experiences yourself. Imagine the sanity of being alive and filled with the love of your existence. This realization will be your Awakening. Because of love, I am shouting my happiness out loud! I can't control it anymore; tears run down my cheek. I love without an object. I am just in love with myself, the world, and the beauty of my existence, and I am Now Here.

I remember making love to her, the carefulness and consideration to please her. Considering the wants and needs of another human being because I was in love.

Will I be able to view another human being the same way again? Yes, when I realize the perfection of the creation of men and women. Will I ever be able to feel Walt Whitman's words of love and tenderness for everybody he encounters? Yes, it has happened to me. I know it now. It sounds silly to love those who deceive you, those who are bickering about you, those who are jealous. But this is

Awakening. You asked for it, and now you must realize that the answer might not please your ego.

Love is not being alone in a dark room, meditating. It is not removing yourself from the world where discrepancies do not reach you. *"Love your neighbor as yourself"* is an ever-lasting proposition leading you into Heaven.

When we are present, we understand that everything is connected and precisely arranged to help us evolve.

When we are in love, we see traces of this understanding and can get a taste of the beauty of life, but there is a catch. For human beings, love does not last. It is given to us to get a taste of the divine. But be prepared to pay as the experience of love will fade away. Often the worldly love will be corrupted and turned into its dark opposite.

In our current state of consciousness, we cannot constantly have positive emotions like love. Positive emotion cannot change. They are here to stay. We are legion; without unity, our love fades away and is replaced by negative feelings and critical perceptions.

I cringe when I hear people utter "love you" without any attention, without the heart involved, just an ordinary word copied and mindlessly expressed.

But I also cringe about myself uttering those exact words, knowing too well that my words are too often not my real feelings.

Remember, the Absolute or God is a universe of Conscious Love. We are his offspring, filled with love, poised to spread it along our way.

Such a high aim to achieve and yet so little will to attain this bliss.

Perceiving real love is reaching God; then, our journey is complete.

This simple statement sums up all the words in this book. Love is the source's source; we are lost in darkness without it. We carry the wisdom in our hearts, and the purity of our minds will use it for our own good and the good of the world.

We need to throw ourselves at the feet of the Beloved and be rewarded with boundless bliss and eternal rest.

You know who your Beloved is; you know it deep in your heart, and the journey you have begun will reveal it with every step. This union is achieved through prayer. Prayer means to be and feel the Presence of Oneself. The virtues that unite our Souls with God are Love, Acceptance, and Remembrance. Be drunk with the Love of God.

Love is not a human desire; it is endless. Human love is like the thirst of a man who drinks salt water: he gets no satisfaction, and his thirst only increases. But real love is enough because it is the union with God, the endless bliss of uniting with one's higher power. We write and sing about love and are mad about love. And yet we have forgotten the true meaning of love. Not loving another human being, not being loved by another human being, but to feel united with the Love of the Universe, with the Love of God, the endless ocean of acceptance and harmony. This is the love you want, and we all search for it.

. . .

In our current existence, we rarely feel real love. Today we love; tomorrow, we hate; and after tomorrow, we forget. We cannot love because we cannot have constant positive emotions. Our emotions and feelings change rapidly; they have no center to hold on to and no permanent endurance in our quest to achieve them. The love blows away with the wind, the rain washes it out, and the sun dries it up.

My greatest feelings of love and remembering my earthly existence were always the moments of Being Present and Awake. Lifting the veil is feeling this endless love, where there is no resentment, and only the beauty of my existence appears.

All spiritual teachings speak and focus on Love. The meaning of love is Presence. One can only love when present to the individual or object in front. Love has been diminished as a fleeting emotion that depends on the atti-tude of the other person we say we love. We only love them when they love us. When they do something we dislike, we stop loving them.

How foolish is this behavior? How easy is it to say "I love You" without understanding the impact this word brings to our life? I chuckle in movies when one person says, "I love you," and the other replies, "Me too." Does this mean they love themself as well? Is it disguising the lie about the real feelings by not saying, "I love you too"?

Love begins with the understanding that we do not have unity. The "I" in "love you" is just part of many personalities that might replace the word "love" with "hate," "dislike," or "despise."

We do not have any permanent positive emotions, and we still believe in the myth of 'never-ending love' by shutting out the reality of our fleeting feelings.

Only Being Present allows one to be in Love. When I am Here Now, the beauty of this world, of human beings in general and especially the person I am close with, becomes apparent and strikingly beautiful.

To learn to love, start with a simple house plant or a small pet, like a fish or turtle. Will I be able to take care of these living organisms constantly? Will I pay attention after the novelty of having them ends? Consistency is the key to love. Love is not just a feeling but rather an effort to keep this emotion alive and to weather any storm that might harm this precious jewel.

Love takes effort and constant care. Being in the Moment is the only way to keep it alive and flourishing. Once you choose to be in the Moment, you become the sage with servitude in your heart. Your heart moves somebody else. The door to the other person's door is closed when your heart is closed. So, bathe the people around you in the sunlight of your spring; you will treasure their being and open their hearts.

"For what is more blessed, worthy of a man, and more like divine goodness than to serve and assist as many as require help." Francesco Petrarcha

Beauty is Presence

≈

"Men must be taught that beauty is a necessity." Plato

Your appreciation of beauty is an essential aspect of Awakening. Our Soul is beautiful and needs its equivalent in the outer world to appear.

My teacher, Robert Burton, often comments about creating one's environment beautiful so the Angels will want to visit.

Beauty and its expression in the outside world are not a question of money, not an aspect of wealth or the ability to purchase things to make something beautiful.

It starts with oneself and one's appearance. Ironing my shirt in the morning is a prayer for embracing the day and appreciating my life. When you go to an important event like a wedding, a job interview, or a date, we understand the importance of grooming ourselves.

Today is essential; it is my only day celebrating my life.

Awakening is so simple. We forget the primary ingredient of our life: Intentionality.

One cannot have beauty without Presence. So be intentional in all that you do to recognize beauty and strive toward it.

I wake up in the morning and take my bed sheet in my hand, lifting it and exposing my body. I look around the room. I notice the dim light, the appearance of shapes in my eyes, and the feeling of thankfulness to experience another day.

I fill the kettle with water, place it on the electric socket, and grind the coffee beans. I pour the boiling water over them. I see my hand holding the kettle's handle and feel its weight and shape. I sense my feet on the ground, the kitchen lamp illuminating my actions. I am here this morning and happy to have appeared again.

Then I lose myself, forgetting about my aim because I am using the bathroom. So, I buffer the business of being human, disguise it with a glance at some phone applications, and then I appear again. I read a poem. I listen to a Cantata by Bach. I have returned to my life, my existence, my Awakening.

Life is a movement and a rest. But we have no time to rest. We need to appear.

. . .

Beauty is the catalyst to appear again and again.

The little flower I put into the vase last evening. My beautiful coffee cup. The red, fiery napkin complements the tablecloth.

Beauty is in us; it does not need any object. We see beauty in our Being. We like specific shapes in women and men; we enjoy different compositions of words and sounds. I salute you for every preference and denial. It is you that can do, achieve, and create. Please pay attention and Be whoever you are; otherwise, it will be discarded in your dreams and lifeless imaginations.

"Today, I discovered that the jewel-like beauty, the presence, is the one we call the Beloved." Rumi

The revelation Rumi gives makes me understand all Sufi poems. The simplicity of Being Present in our life is the call for the Beloved. Rumi says in another verse: *"You may not know yet, but you will when grief disappears."*

The beauty of our life is always with us. It is our guiding light amidst the darkness of sleep and identification, elevating us from the prison's dungeon. The goal is your beauty - all else is pretense. And this beauty is not complicated; it depends on simplicity. The simplicity of harmony and grace, the rhythm of style and heart.

Lift your heart and see your beauty. Nothing is easier said and hard to be done in our complicated, multifaceted world that sees beauty only in the famed creations of celebrities and artists. But know that you are the artist of your life. You create your existence; make it a beautiful one, a life to remember, the one you have now. Do not waste it on idle considerations.

One beautiful love poem comes from the English poet Elizabeth Barrett Browning:

> *"How do I love thee? Let me count the ways. I love thee to the depth, breadth, and height my Soul can reach when feeling out of sight. For the ends of ideal Beauty and ideal Grace."*

But words cannot tell of the divine beauty, no matter how skilled the poet is. Heavenly things do not need words; they penetrate us directly and envelope us in their realm of harmonious silence.

One cannot behold God with the eye of reason. Only the look of the heart can see it. So allow your Presence to make you beautiful within. Beauty surrounds us, but we can only perceive it through supportive circumstances, like wandering in a garden or seeing a rainbow. Striving for our inner beauty is the only assurance to keep it alive among the quick fading of likes and dislikes.

We often dismiss the beauty of our lives. We identify our shortcomings and downfalls with a life wasted or unfulfilled. If we understand the guidance of Higher Forces* in our lives, we know that all these problematic endeavors are here to remind us and are made to lead us into Being.

Do not judge your life as meaningless and wasted because you missed a turn; you were denied a possibility. It is all arranged for you to realize your life; nothing is wasted in this universe. The angels will not give up on you; they know what you need to awaken. Beauty is within you, and they show it to you by making you suffer, by doubting yourself. Come back to the Moment. Be here. Create the space inside of you that understands stillness. Presence brings inner joy. It harmonizes with the simplicity of the Moment outside. It does not need form or possessions. The beauty you seek does not exist in objects but within you.

"I have served beauty. Is there anything greater in the world?" Sappho

The Spiritual Truth About Life

~

"Nothing beautiful without struggle." Plato

I t is impossible to let go of the attachments to things. This is ingrained into our existence as humans. Only when we stop seeking our identifications and understand the permanent race of the *lower self** can we start to see it.

First, try to observe it. Then, stop trying to change things that cannot be changed. Instead, bring light to the automatic processes of your ego. By seeing oneself identified with something, the attachment is not more total. Transformation starts when you realize you are not what you see but what sees. This awareness is the beginning of Spiritual Consciousness.

. . .

The identification of having something can only be sustained for a short time. The need to have must be fed by more external things to keep the illusion alive. To have is the fiction of the ego by pretending to create identity and permanency to make itself unique.

The quest for more leaves us restless and unsatisfied in our lives. To enjoy things is more important than to Be. We become addicted to this quest. Most people want conflicting things. At times, different and opposing identifications pop up. But this typically never includes being in this Moment, just being here. Restlessness, boredom, and anxiety replace it. There can only be fulfillment if the wanting structure is replaced with a new sense of Being. The greed of the lower self* makes people ruthless in obtaining their shallow wants and haves.

Our false personality always wonders how to get away from the present Moment; the true Self is happy just to be in this Moment, without wishing it to be different, and just accepting it regardless.

The true Self requires no naming, just listening, looking, and perceiving.

In the profound quiet, the beauty of our life comes into view.

To be present is to have a perfect vision. The divine momentum of your efforts shows in your life unfolding.

We are two in one. The most significant contradiction in the universe. An angel and a devil in the same vessel.

You understand your life's real story when you see the

angel caught in a body of decay and sleep. So, appear more and more and shed the vessel of oblivion. Reveal Your Higher Self* by itself. The sun shines through the dark clouds. Sweet is to use the forces of adversity. Transforming your suffering will bring joy and true beauty, the bliss of existing.

True beauty does not depend on outside appearance. It just is.

Having the power to experience reality, who would choose imagination?

Do not depend on words and letters that wish for imagination; rely on your waking moments.

"Easy Going"— what a concept leading you into sleep. Awakening is work and effort. Sleep proposes leading an easy life, an existence of pleasure and abundance without hard work. For example, you become a millionaire at thirty years of age and then relax and enjoy the joys of life. What will it bring? Will money be the answer? Will you be happy driving around in a fancy convertible? Will there be lasting happiness in ordering any dish on the menu without looking at the price?

You know the answer already. Money does not make us happy, and there cannot be paradise besides our inner awareness of God's Presence within.

This leads to the fact that what we give returns to us. If I give hate, I will receive hate. If I give love, I will receive love.

We all have a powerful tool in our heads: our minds. However, scientists estimate that humans only use a tiny fraction of their brain's capabilities. For example, it is known that the brain only weighs about 3% to 4% of our body's weight but consumes approximately 1/3rd of all the energy we give to our body.

Use your mind to imagine your Presence. Many people promote the idea that you can imagine wealth and outward success. If this is what you want, go ahead. But imagine your Awakening instead if you wish to Be Present, be more aware, and feel God's love upon you. You have the choice.

Johan Wolfgang von Goethe answered these choices long ago in his metaphysical work "Faust": *"Richness or Understanding; Seeing or Being."*

Our minds and hearts are very closely connected. Our words and thoughts will manifest in our hearts and living reality. We decide on our terms and with our ideas which we are.

Plato says that we all have a *"Divine Design"* in us. Our life can unfold along this design of Higher Forces*, reaching the ideal state destined for us. Most women and men do not follow their higher purpose. Many refuse to acknowledge it, and those who find it feasible do not know where and how to start.

It starts with being intentional. It begins with the right attitudes and creating the "right" wishes. However, we must first be careful with our words. What we say will manifest in our lives. Our words, feelings, and actions must come from a sincere place inside us to find life's true meaning. A fleeting thought of wishing for something, a half-baked attempt to achieve an aim, will only lead to nothing.

Furthermore, scientists have also discovered that humans have about 70,000 thoughts per day. Interestingly, only 5% of them are generally new. Our thoughts go along the usual ways, the beaten path of our mind, the well-known landscape of our imagination.

How about smashing these old tapes? How about playing a new song of love, a new symphony of happiness, a concert of acceptance?

But fear blocks everything. Fear of the unknown, of not making ends meet, of poverty, of other people's opinions, judgments, and of our own defeat.

Fear is nothing but fear itself. Why worry? The worries that cause distress will never happen. Instead, establish deep in your heart the conviction that only good can come into your life. You are made in God's image; he sees only beauty in you. The bad and the evil are only man's creations of losing faith in a rewarding and harmonious existence.

Now is the time to escape that wheel of misery and find your true calling. Prepare yourself for what must surely come. Prepare yourself by wishing for a life full of wonders, love, and happiness. Remember that You, with God, are a majority.

Replace the word God with any other entity you call the miracle of this world. For me, they are Higher Forces*. By relating to something higher, I elevate myself. I remember that these forces do not like to come to me when I am shouting, cursing, or judging, but only in the calm moments of remembering myself and being in harmony with the world around me.

> *"To see a World in a Grain of Sand*
> *And a Heaven in a Wild Flower,*
> *Hold Infinity in the palm of your hand*
> *And Eternity in an hour."*
> *William Blake*

We need to hold on to our vision on our way to achieving these states of Spiritual Consciousness. Be happy with your small victories: You dismiss a colleague's off comment and reject the negativity that appears in you. You stand in the overcrowded subway and are not miserable. You are unconcerned about the coffee you spilled on your shirt. These achievements are our milestones, our measure of evolution.

Give up the judgments and worldly standards and come back to reality. Love is real. This Moment is real. You know it, I know it; this miracle binds us together. You are what you are. Do not despair. Enjoy your current life, knowing that living right will lead you to the next level and, one day, to paradise. My response to anything and anybody is creating my world. I hold on to my vision, and I'm not discouraged by an occasional slip or a moment of sleep.

"Carefully watch your thoughts, for they become your words. Manage and watch your words, for they will become your actions. Consider and judge your actions, for they have become your habits. Acknowledge and watch your habits, for they shall become your values. Understand and embrace your values, for they become your destiny."
Mahatma Gandhi

The Story of the Three Laughing Monks

"I have heard about three monks. No names are mentioned because they never disclosed their names to anybody. They never answered anything. In China, they were known as the three laughing monks. And they did only one thing: they would enter a village, stand in the marketplace, and start laughing. They would laugh with their whole being, and suddenly, people would become aware of them. Then onlookers would also get the infection, and a crowd would gather. What was happening? Eventually, the entire village would start laughing just because of the monks. Everybody would get involved. Once that happened, the monks would move to another city.

They were loved very much. That was their only sermon, their only message: laugh. They would not teach, only laugh. In time, they became famous all over the country; they were called the "Three Laughing Monks." All of China loved them and respected them. Nobody had ever preached in such a way that life must be just laughter and nothing else. They were not laughing at anyone. They were laughing as if they had understood the cosmic joke. And they spread so much joy all over China without using a single word. People would ask for their names, but they would simply laugh. They were just the "Three Laughing Monks."

Then they grew old. And while staying in a single village, one of the three monks died. The whole village gathered. The town became curious because they thought that the other two would indeed weep when one of them died. But the two monks stood beside the corpse of the third and laughed— such a belly of a laugh. So, the villagers asked them to explain this. For the first time, the two monks spoke: 'We are laughing because this man has won. We always wondered who would die first, and this man defeated us. We are laughing at our defeat and his victory. Also, he lived with us for many years, and we laughed together and enjoyed each other's togetherness and Presence. There can be no better way of giving him the last send-off. We can only laugh.'

But the whole village was sad. And when the dead monk's body was put on the funeral pyre, the town realized that the remaining two monks were not the only ones joking; the dead one was also laughing! He had asked his companions not to change his clothes. It was conventional that they change his dress and bathe the body when a man died. But the third monk had said, 'Don't bathe me because I have never been unclean. So much laughter has been in my life that no impurity can come to me. I have not gathered any dust. Laughter is always young and fresh. So don't bathe me, and don't change my clothes.' So, to respect his wishes, they did not change his clothes or bathe him.

And when they put the body on fire, the Chinese fireworks under his clothes went off. The village laughed, and the other two monks said, 'You rascal. You are dead and yet defeated us once again. Your laughter is the last laugh.'"

The Big Lie

~

"Everything that irritates us about others can lead us to an understanding of ourselves." Carl Gustav Jung

The ego is a net of recurring thoughts and emotions that give us the identification of "I." It is the imaginary idea of who we think we are.

Spiritual Consciousness is not thinking. It is the awareness of "I am thinking." Our mind or capability to think is a function, like touching a fabric or hearing a sound. Spiritual Consciousness is being aware of these functions in oneself but not being a part of them. Spiritual Consciousness allows us to perceive "I am" separately from our functions. It exists separately from our body; therefore, it can survive our physical death.

Your true identity is Spiritual Consciousness itself, not the identifications of your ego. There is no form attached to our Being. The ultimate truth of who we are is not what we possess or think but the perception of "I am."

Many people are identified by the voice in their head, with its binding force to identifications, judgments, and opinions. People unaware of this believe these expressions are who they are. Their mind is stamped with the perception of "I." This doesn't allow separation to occur, and understanding reality is impossible. The ego has fortified itself against any possibility of seeing reality as it is. The ego creates a closed sleep circuit, denying anything outside the borders of form and matter.

To form this closed circuit, the *lower self** uses its preferred elements: judgment and complaints. It thrives with aggressive shouting, name-calling, and physical violence.

Resentment is an emotion strongly connected to complaining. It feeds from the labeling of people and provides energy to the lower self*. Resentment is feeling bitter, offended, aggrieved, or disappointed. We resent other people's dishonesty, greed, lack of integrity, and lies. Our ego loves it. Instead of accepting unconsciousness in others - seeing our own unconscious actions - we stamp them permanently with their faults. The faults we perceive in others might not even be there; it merely reflects our judgment. A projection of our mind to see enemies and make us superior.

. . .

The words I speak are the words I live by. Outside my own conscious awareness, there is no experience, a non-reaction.

Non-reaction to the ego of somebody is strength, not weakness. Non-reaction is forgiveness. Complaining is the negativity that the ego exudes. Instead of focusing on that, look at your Consciousness. Ego and Being Present cannot exist together.

Complaining strengthens the ego. To carry a grievance is a long-standing resentment. Forgiveness can happen when you acknowledge your grievance and understand the baggage of old thoughts and emotions. Complaining gives the lower self* superiority. Wanting to be right strengthens it.

The ego knows only me, I, and mine. It takes everything personally.

The false personality is a master of selective and distorted perception. I am right, and you are wrong. Righteousness is more important than human life.

Remember, the truth is just a bundle of thoughts. A subjective interpretation of events. Thoughts can never be the truth; people cannot grasp that different facts exist on different levels.

Only realizing "I am" comes close to the eternal truth of existence. Jesus said: *"I am the way and the truth and the life."* When he speaks about "I am," he refers to the essence of identity in every woman and man.

This is what the gnostic Christian writings mean by "Christ within."

If you are in touch with this inner truth, you are in contact with the infinite Consciousness in this world, the meaning of life.

The truth within is love.

The false personality is the complete identification with thoughts and emotions. It makes what is actually crazy "normal."

Everything you dislike in another person is also in you. Reacting with anger to somebody else's ego shows the same patterns in you. Anything that you resent in the other person is in you as well.

The lower self* is the insanity of the human mind.

Recognize the ego for what it is, and you will be more able to not react and fall into the trap of taking it seriously. The false personality is just an insane illusion of intense thoughts and emotions that sees other people as adversaries, as competition.

Compassion arises when you realize that everybody suffers from the insanity of their mind. Reactivity is the fuel that keeps this insanity alive. Non-reaction is peace; to react is drama, war, and negativity.

When you sit still, as if meditating, you are exposed to your ego's forces. All kinds of crazy thoughts will rush into your mind. The mind takes you on a rollercoaster without rhyme or reason. You see the craziness inside; the voice does not stop. It talks about resentment, being hurt, and being mistreated. It will imagine how to pay back these people with clever moves. Your lower self* might imagine all the benefits you will reap soon, the excellent behavior you displayed recently, or the wonderfulness of your actions. Your ego is just a wild animal, insane and lunatic.

When you negatively interact with others, like

disputing over ideas, experiencing threats, or even physical violence, your false personality becomes even more antici- pated. It rushes to attack; it insults and blames without knowing the consequences. A madman in a mad universe is mad at other mad people.

Are you able to wake up a little during these moments? Can you stop reacting? Can you create a small space within you where all this madness does not touch? Allowing for this conscious effort will try to replace the ego with your Higher Self*. To love thy enemies. To forgive those who hurt you. To be not touched by the world. This is when you become free.

Let go of the drama between false personalities. Choose the peace inside of yourself and find your conscience. Understand the turmoil in other people and have mercy on them. They suffer from being unable to let go of their resentment and anger.

Beyond your ego lies your true identity. When you start tasting the sweetness of not reacting, of not allowing your mind to go crazy, the *lower self** loses its grip on you. The beginning is to observe this. To see the ego for what it is: a lie you have told yourself all these years.

"To understand reality, you have to be present." Robert Burton

The Way of the Warrior

∼

"The language of truth is simple." Euripides

I create every Moment of my Life. I am not a victim; whatever I have chosen becomes my reality.

Who we think we are and what kind of convictions we carry in our heart defines the outcomes in our life. It is a simple equation, and facing this truth is the first step toward Awakening.

There is nothing noble in suffering, nothing noble in being the victim.

"Remember you are not a crow, but the mystic osprey that never needs to light," says Rumi, "then you can be walking with Shams."

. . .

I remember my self-afflicted suffering, dwelling in the sweetness of grief and feeling abandoned by the Gods. I was lying for days in a darkened room in sunny Miami Beach, Florida, banning the sunshine from healing my suffering. Occasionally, I would get up to go to the fridge to make another gin and tonic, giving in to my self-pity, the misery of my life. How pathetic, how tragic; my *lower self** enjoyed the suffering as something noble, something aristocratic. How much trash can a sick mind create? How many excuses can a weak, lost man invent to feel sorrow for his life?

I am German and know the "Weltschmerz" attitude too well. Although the ingrained German approach to life is heavy and complex, this was pure self-pity.

Would live in North America, the land of easy-going convenience and wealth, be capable of casting away any desperation and negativity towards me?

No matter where we are and who we are, we experience these moments of despair and dark clouds that can suddenly appear and stay for hours or days.

The way of the warrior is a simple, straightforward way. This way does not know the word "trying." Either I do, or I don't. This way does not know the word "can't."

I choose to or choose not to. Awakening means growing up to take responsibility for one's life. Keeping one's commitments, taking one's word as law, and speaking the truth with compassion are simple concepts of some-body real.

Another essential aspect of the warrior way is "not to inner consider." Inner consideration is always concerned with the judgment of others and how people see us. Do they approve of me?

These worries take so much energy away from us. It creates fear and insecurity. We need to replace this negative emotion against ourselves with something that uplifts us, with something higher that brings out the good in us.

We can call this "external consideration."

Instead of taking oneself as the middle of the universe by asking what people are thinking of us, if we dress appropriately, or if we behave by the norm, we put the other person in focus. We ask what we can do for them. External consideration is an expression of love and care; I am not more concerned about my imaginary picture or the spot on my shirt or my hair not looking perfect; instead, I am focusing on another person's need or wish.

External consideration makes us God-like; it is the basis for the care and love for other people, and by doing it, one becomes present, aware of the Moment, happy, and joyful. One cannot feel and perceive another person's needs unless one is present. It is so much more beautiful to give than to receive.

As Walt Whitman observed, the reflection of giving and coming back to the giver unfolds into a beautiful interaction between human beings. Mechanically, mothers have external considerations but have no way to act differently; they have no choice, like an animal's intuitive care for its offspring.

In life-and-death situations, we can find people who overcome their fear of rescuing a stranger, often giving their own life for the survival of somebody else. These are extreme examples.

I am talking more about the small, inconspicuous things we can do to consider somebody and not be noticed. Because so often, the noticing, the pointing out, brings vanity and destroys the kind act with praise and admiration.

I am talking about waiting to be served until everybody else has been served, taking white meat instead of a leg because it is somebody else's favorite. Carrying groceries from the car, watching a movie the other person wanted to see instead of the one I preferred, taking a trip to the lake instead of the mountain, and listening to a specific piece of music while knowing the other person likes it. You understand what I mean.

The secret is to do it inconspicuously, not taking any credit for it and especially not bragging about it. The way of the warrior is a simple, straightforward way. With it, one can achieve change. Being willing to do what is hard, doing it at 100%, taking no shortcuts, speaking the truth, and never giving up are the ingredients to succeed in The Art to Be Here Now.

"The ideal day will never come. The ideal day is today when we make it so." Horace

Creating Positive Habits - Octaves

~

"Do small things as if they were great." Heraclites

Anyone can devise a simple ritual and integrate it into their day, week, or month. In Zen monasteries, even ordinary activities, like bathing and eating, are ritualized and have the complete attention of the practitioners.

Ritualizing daily tasks encourages a mindful approach to your life, imbuing it with a powerful transformational ethos. It can be as simple as walking at a specific time of day, eating only with a knife and fork, and drinking out of a glass, not a bottle. Your inner change will occur when you repeat these reminders constantly. Practice makes the master. For outsiders, your ritual might seem overly simplistic or even fruitless. However, when you engage your habits with attention, you will understand that it brings

Presence into your life, a space to rely upon, and moments to remember.

A slight change in your habits can guide your life to a different destination. Making a choice slightly better than what you are used to will make a significant difference in your life. We must use common sense and avoid worries, fear, and self-pity.

Reading something inspiring, visiting a friend, or caring for someone else will help you stop over self-indulging.

Your success is the product of your daily habits; your choices define the difference between who you are and who you could be.

No matter where you are in your life, even changing a small ordinary habit will put you on the path to success. So be concerned with your trajectory rather than with your current results.

Your habits measure your outcome. You get what you repeat and what you have in your focus - a simple truth yet a reality that creates love, harmony, and success.

Paying attention also allows one to discover what is happening to oneself. What are the cravings and desires that rule my life? Lifting the veil of imaginary ideas and capabilities is crucial, allowing the curtains to open before your eyes to see who you are. When this occurs, you start your awareness and understanding of yourself.

Look at your little daily choices. They add up over days, weeks, and months. Good habits are your ally; bad habits are your enemy. Stay encouraged even during the setbacks that occur from time to time. So many vows have been broken. It is not about the grand aspirations; it is returning to the small things that make this life great.

Subscribe to the Word of the Day; study one new idea daily. Get up five minutes earlier to read a poem before you make coffee. Start your day with a short sequence of yoga poses, and while driving in your car to work, laugh out loud for one minute.

Breakthrough moments are only the result of previous actions. They are a build-up of prior efforts that come to fruition suddenly. Then, finally, the rainbow appears, sunshine peeking through the clouds and the rays hitting the spot where you are sitting. Then you'll know you crossed the critical threshold to unleash a significant shift.

Along the process of change, there are specific intervals. All our actions, ventures, and projects can be called "Octaves." Anything unfolding in our lives follows the same pattern discovered in the musical octave. Every octave has two points where something can change; something must happen at these specific points to continue the path.

These points are called intervals and appear in a musical octave between the Mi - Fa and the Si - Do.

Comparing it to a musical octave in all our activities allows us to experience these two intervals as obstacles in completing our aims.

The Musical Octave

Do - Re - Mi *Interval* **Fa - Sol - La - Si** *Interval* **Do**

An example

We invited friends to our house and had a wonderful dinner. After they left, I wanted to clean up and wash dishes. In the beginning, I felt good. The dinner had given me energy, so I put on my favorite Chet Baker record to keep me in a positive mood. The "Do" of the octave "Cleaning-Up" was strong and made the chore easy. I reached Re quickly and made it with enthusiasm to Mi. All plates and glasses were washed. But oh my god, I forgot to wash the pots and pans! By then, I felt tired; my energy grew weaker.

Many people would drop out at this point. Their will – a term we will define in a later chapter – is not strong enough to continue cleaning the pots and pans. So instead, they will say, "I will finish cleaning up tomorrow morning."

But then my wife entered the kitchen, gave me a big kiss and hug, and I felt a little stronger again. I changed the disc, selected some R&B, and moved in the new rhythm through the pots. I bridged this first interval by putting some different energy into my work, getting help from the outside (my wife), and understanding that I do not have time tomorrow morning to clean because I have an important meeting at my job.

. . .

I sailed through Fa- Sol - La and arrived at the Si - Do, the last step to finish my octave. Putting away the pots and pans meant my work was complete, but this was not the end. Next, I must rinse and wipe down the sink, hang the towels and rags, clean the floor, and put away my apron. And then, to my dismay, my wife came into the kitchen again with two glasses she had forgotten to bring in earlier. I wanted to place them in the sink to let them sit for my wife to do tomorrow.

At this point, I needed all my strength. I needed to understand that cleaning those last two glasses meant creating a will, not being defeated by the *lower self** that would instead go to bed and make love to my wife (I deserved it, right?). I had to remind myself: who am I? Do I quit because I am tired? Do I walk away and forget about it?

This simple example of an evening with friends at home and the cleaning afterward is the real test of how strong my will is and how much I understand Awakening.

Only by finishing the small things can I tackle the big stuff.

Awakening is big. It is the biggest and most important thing a human being can do. It goes against all odds, against all current mechanical streams in life that want to keep us bound and locked in the prison of sleep.

The Hidden Patterns of Self Destruction

Why do we sabotage ourselves?
Why is it that people procrastinate?
Why do so many people fail despite all the chances and
possibilities?

We live in a time full of more opportunities and resources than ever. Most of us have access to all modern tools, yet we cannot use them positively and fruitfully for our life aspirations.

Think about some successful people who had no resources at all. People born handicapped, like Helen Keller, or born into slavery, like Frederick Douglas. Yet, against all the odds, they created magic for all of us.

We can learn how to take away our excuses from these people. To remove the negative mindset that tells us we cannot fulfill our life's dreams and aspirations.

As human beings, our nervous system is hard-wired for comfort. But changing this programming for growth makes us who we can become.

Manage a dynamic tension between comfort and growth, pleasure and work. This struggle is a constant source of frustration for many people.

When you start to make changes, you are excited. The energy of the beginning takes you magically to a certain point, and then it becomes problematic. You are wondering why you chose it. The energy from the emphatic start is now used up, so you must find a new force to support your efforts. You may feel stuck in place; you cannot see any changes. This just means you are still determining your aim. Remember that the most effective outcomes are delayed.

Therefore, creating long-lasting habits and routines that will help you achieve your goals and better your life is challenging. You made a few little changes but could not see any tangible results. Unfortunately, most people stop just before the results appear. Tragedy has it that progress is lost in despair and self-doubt.

But persistence is the key to any change. Small but continuous efforts bring results. We look at the Grand Canyon and know that the Colorado River needed millions of years to dig out stone millimeter by millimeter. Still, we must understand how to apply this knowledge to our lives and efforts.

Our bad habits of complaining and doubting will kick in occasionally, holding us back from our rightly deserved aim. We are God in human form and must strive for perfection by transforming our human existence and dream-like state.

Remember to tell yourself every morning, *"I can do it because I can."*

Mastery requires patience and persistence. We all know this, but truly understanding it requires a mental and emotional effort to make it ourselves. Have you seen Michelangelo's Sistine Chapel in Rome or the Great Cheops Pyramid in Egypt? What does it take to accept that outstanding achievements take time? They are labors of love because love conquers all. They grab attention and excellence to exist beyond the stars.

. . .

The stars, the whole Universe, is mechanical. Billions of stars follow the mechanical laws of the Universe. But our conscious achievements go further; they are not automatic but a breath of God. Your life is excellent; it is your only one, so make it unique. All big things come from small beginnings.

Building a good habit, a wholesome routine, is like cultivating a precious flower. Use care and attention with daily efforts and know-how.

Set specific, attainable goals. Experiencing success in your everyday achievements will strengthen your will and dedication. We all deal with setbacks along the way toward succeeding in our plans. We must find our scientific system to help us achieve our aims. We are all human beings and function in similar ways. We change bit by bit.

The Strength of Prayers

Do you believe in God, a Higher Power, an Omnipotent Presence? Then learn to speak to this Entity and tell her your hopes, dreams, and aspirations. Tell her your heart. She will not judge you. Instead, she will embrace you by opening the channel to your understanding. We must voice our feelings and taste them. Hear them with our ears to distinguish their specific sound and listen to the fragrance.

As the medieval German Mystic, Meister Eckhart, voiced:

"If your prayer is Thank You – it is enough."

What You Focus on Expands

It is called the "strangest secret." Yet, it is known that what we think about, imagine, and dream about will become accurate and true.

This observation is self-evident, yet it takes tremendous effort to introduce this concept into our lives.

Do not focus on harmful elements in life; otherwise, you will be in many ways lost, like the junkie who shoots poison into his veins, the alcoholic who chugs down the liquor, or the suicidal person standing on the ledge of a bridge.

Our life is beautiful. Seeing it takes the correct focus point and perspective. My belief is the sum of my verifications and understandings.

We all have verified the beauty of our existence. The sun rays through our window, the whiff of lilac in the field, the jump into the lake on a hot July afternoon, the holding of hands with the beloved, seeing a butterfly emerge from its chrysalis, the baby's smile recognizing her mother.

When you remember these beautiful encounters and keep them close to your heart, you cannot be misled.

Love Yourself

How can I love myself? I see all my shortcomings, anger, rage, and judgments. And yet, I know that I have been given this life and body to evolve. Remember, nobody is your friend, nobody is your enemy, they are your teachers. We need to be taught to love.

I was loved by women who knew my faults, loved by my

mother, who beat me for not living up to her expectations, and loved by a friend who competed with me fiercely in all aspects of life.

Now I can see it more clearly. I can see the love beyond the insulting words, the fear, the jealousy, and the resentment. I beg to give up my grievances and the judgments of other people because I am judging myself. To love is to be God. Love does not ask for what it brings or its reward; it just exists.

I know I am far away from this love, yet I understand that my grief is disappearing; it is replaced by the joy of having found the meaning of my life. Love is not a feeling. It is my home, my destination.

Forgive Yourself

I remember the moments when I did something so embarrassing and inhumane that it still haunts me today. I remember the moments when I lied to women for sex; I recall the times stealing and lying, and I repented the moments when I was full of hate and resentment for the success of others. At this moment, I must forgive myself for all the wrongs I have done.

There was the time I scolded my father because of his dirty fingernails at my sporting event, a game of Handball. I will never forget this Moment of pain and despair when he left the arena because of my hurting words.

My quest for forgiveness stems from this Moment of Conscience, my first Moment of Awakening. I know you have this Moment too. It is when your Soul appears that your God-like essence shall show itself. The shame is your victory, the tears are your pearls, and the Moment is forever yours. When you remember this Moment, you are the person you want to become—filled with compassion, ready to love. Understanding that life carries pain and suffering is the key to your happiness. Beyond all this is the bliss of waking up and being present in one's own life.

Do Not Judge Yourself

To judge is to limit yourself to the past.

Just remember a politician on trial saying, with his counselor's advice, that he does not recognize the incident. Who did what? It was not his Higher Self* that committed the crime; it was not his Soul that got upset; it was not his God-like Being that got negative.

Separate yourself from the expressions of your lower aspects. Instead, focus on the ones you like to develop. Inhale the oxygen of life, the rays of love. For example, in my car driving, I often use a mantra to relieve myself of life's negative aspects: *"I replace my resentment with gratitude and kindness."*

Moments of understanding are often filled with tears and wailing. Tears are necessary; they wash away the particles in your eyes when you put your head too deep in the sand.

Sometimes I resent others, thinking they had luck, success, and the life I wanted. I did not realize that their suffering and despair spoke louder than any appearance. These simple sentences in life that are common knowledge, like *"the grass is not greener on the other side,"* are tidbits of conscious knowledge, and taking them truthfully will change our life.

Attract Positive Thoughts

Much is written about the Law of Attraction. But how do we live it? For example, does it make a difference if we repeat a sentence daily without feeling it, believing it, or being it?

I tried myself daily, tried to chisel a thought into reality, and be the man I wanted to be. Yet it does not happen overnight, it does not happen instantly, and it does not occur without effort.

Living in this new online world of instant gratifications, I understand the programming that happened to us. Now you can become anybody in a few weeks, achieve fame overnight, reap benefits instantly, and get the ordered online item within one day.

This is the illusion of our life today. I do not want to dwell on forgotten memories of receiving a word from a loved one traveling after weeks, or waiting for a book with anticipation in the snail mail.

But I do know that positive thoughts create positive experiences. An attitude of joy and love makes joy and love. A vile idea of anger and hate will create a likeness in the thinker. You are what you think. You are what you focus on. Just be a little patient. Refrain from believing that

Heaven is working like an online store. *"Good things come to those who wait"* is another well-known aphorism. You know it is the truth; it cannot be otherwise.

Focus on What You Can Control

What can we control? Do you control the weather? Do you control the timing of the bus's arrival? Do you control the stock market?

You know the answers, yet you still want to control things beyond your control. Why is the obvious so challenging to understand? Why is it that we behave like toddlers? Why do we allow ourselves to be so far from the truth? Trying to find the answers is part of the quest to see reality and the ability to change.

"Men think, and God decides." Understanding our life as a journey into Being, a love story, and an epic poem is essential. Remember, you are not controlling your thoughts; they come and go, but by how you handle your reaction. You can approve or dismiss anything that comes your way by choosing the right path. I'll meet you there.

> *"And I call to mankind: be not curious about God. I am at peace about God ... I hear and behold God in every object. Why should I wish to see God better than this day? I see something of God in each hour of the twenty-four. In the faces of men and women, I see God, and in my own face in the Glass." Walt Whitman*

Attitude and Emotional Understanding

~

"Those who listen to the music of the holy teaching are led into perfect peace." Buddha

W hen we work on ourselves, we often come to a new and deeper understanding of ideas that we were familiar with. One idea that became new and revealing to me is the concept of attitudes. A slight shift in my habitual mental position toward people changed the way of my reactions in life entirely. Many of my attitudes were programmed in me through my parents and my social interactions while growing up. Absorbing these old influences seems like a fate we accept, never asking about the quality and righteousness of these attitudes.

. . .

Coming from a working-class background, the attitudes my parents instilled in me were those of hard work, fear of poverty, and that the riches are for others. The consequences of this programming were also visible in my attitude toward Awakening. I believed this was for somebody else, somebody with better qualities than me, somebody who could speak well, and somebody who walked confidently through life.

Now my attitude has changed. Awakening is for me, has been for me, and unfolded for me, despite many functional flaws. Maybe even because of them, but for sure, despite them.

Spiritual Consciousness does not depend on functions or programming. To be Present does not depend on our body's shape, our mind's agility, or the ability to remember facts.

When we are more present, we can choose our attitudes intentionally. We become an artist with a sophisticated toolkit. We understand if a specific situation needs a strong or a gentle response.

To solve a problem, we need to find the right attitude, the decision on which perspective to choose lies in your aim. Therefore, you must be intentional and aware of your action's consequences for your Awakening.

But first and foremost, we need to understand that our thoughts and attitudes are not real. We can change them following our aim. We use them as a tool for doing something intentionally for our vision.

Our attitudes can never be holy or eternal. Nevertheless, we apply them to our life, intending to reflect our values and verifications. You may not like to offer your left cheek after being slapped on the right one, but you can walk away without a grudge. You can avoid a heated discussion about unimportant topics so as not to identify and keep your mind calm and focused. You may see an unfortunate occurrence as a blessing instead of a curse.

Experiment with your attitudes. Learn how to adopt the right ones to further your aim. Above all, realize that nothing is real in this life unless you add Presence to it - then your attitude will be correct.

We will all have trials on our path to test us and to reveal where our weaknesses are. With the right attitude, we will view our downfall as an opportunity to offer *Higher Forces** a sacrifice of praise. We will see it as divine play. We are the leading actor.

Be aware that temptations come in many forms. Humility opposes pride, meekness conquers anger, charity stifles envy, love wipes out hate, and acceptance deflects suffering. Our temptations are our way out of prison by seeing them and accepting them as part of our human existence.

Creating a positive attitude toward ourselves, our efforts, and the world is essential to Awakening and will allow us to fight such temptations. Nothing that happens to us is neither good nor bad. Our interpretations make them so. It is our choice. Choosing the thoughts that your life is unfolding along your spiritual development is more appropriate for our aim than imagining that the world is conspiring against us with excessive cruelties.

Remember that the friction you are receiving is not because you are bad but because the Gods want you to transform your suffering into Being.

On our journey of Awakening, we gather Emotional Understanding. Emotional Understanding is the realization that our life events might appear damaging or even devastating. However, after some time, we realized these events helped us move on and improve our lives.

I gained Emotional Understanding for the first time while working in Germany as a Public Relations writer for an advertising agency. I got hired to market the formerly state-owned telecommunication company's "Going Public" Event. Anybody who has ever worked in an advertising agency knows the working hours are gruesome.

One evening a week, I would gather with like-minded people to share our experiences and support our efforts to Be Present. So, on this day of the week, a late meeting was scheduled at the agency, and I chose not to go but rather to meet my friends. Having had difficulties with my boss due to mechanical animosity, I feared some recriminations. But it was worse than expected. When I arrived at the office the following day, I was asked to clear my desk within thirty minutes: I was fired.

At the time, fearful emotions and remorseful thoughts rushed into my head and heart. Being fired would mean the end of my career in Germany. I just got a new apartment, but how should I pay the rent now? I felt devastated and beaten.

After a few days of mental suffering, I talked to one of my friends, and he stated, "You are free now; you can go to California to be with your teacher. Isn't this what you always wanted to do?"

YES! He was right. So, I bought an airplane ticket, flew a few weeks later to California, and spent the next few years closely connected to my teacher. I was part of his inner circle.

Being fired was the best thing that could have happened to me. It was a "Kairos" time for me, a time when change can happen, and the Angles helped me with a little push to get me on my way.

Afterward, there were many other moments when I realized that unfortunate, bad, or devastating events could bring quite satisfying results. This Emotional Understanding has calmed my reactions to the events that occur in my life; it has made me understand that my life is unfolding according to my inner journey.

Many people understand the difference between a positive mental attitude and a negative mental attitude. A positive mental attitude is part of the Emotional Understanding of one's play and its different scenes with funny, sad, or exciting undertones. Another example of a recent experience might reveal the differences more clearly.

I purchased a few Options Call Contracts, betting on the rise of the US Dollar against the European Currency, the Euro. These contracts did not do well; they would expire worthlessly on the expiration day. But the Market turned on the last day, and suddenly these Call Options were "in the money." I would have to sell them before the Stock Exchange closed not to have to buy the underlying stocks. I was away on this day and didn't anticipate this move; I didn't check my positions. So when Monday morning came, I received an email informing me that I had a huge margin call to settle because the Brokerage Firm had automatically purchased the underlying stocks for me.

There was a time in my life when I would have been horrified at the thought of being responsible for coming up with thousands of dollars to pay for the transaction. It was money I did not have, money I could not borrow. I would have to sell my car to do it.

But at this point in my life, I already had a positive attitude toward anything that came my way. So, I told myself that this move was the best thing to have happened. The stocks will rise more this Monday trading day, and the Gods are giving me a little bonus.

And so, it happened. When I called the brokerage firm to discuss my options, I was told that I had to sell the stocks today, but because the Market had made another big jump, I would gain a hefty profit.

We can choose to think with a negative attitude or a positive attitude. Life has taught me that thinking positively about an unclear event usually turns positive and beneficial. Try it. Just shift from a negative mindset to a positive attitude and see things happening for you.

This attitude is essential in our spiritual journey. From time to time, we will experience setbacks and defeat. We will step off the path and find ourselves disoriented and lost.

But with the right attitude, these experiences will nourish our evolution. These experiences are happening to help us grow. By realizing the true nature of things, we can look at our life with a dispassionate attitude.

Do not resist what happens to you. The Gods arranged it to make you see and understand. Bad turns into good with the power of non-resistance.

Always do what the present moment requires, and you'll learn how to decide what relationship you want to have with the Present. Then, confirm this relationship as often as possible because you will forget. Your mind will take you hostage to identify with your life and forget your vows. Your mind tricks you when it suggests that all is bad and unfortunate. Remember that your interpretations of your current situation are subjective. Come back to the realization of being here now and that your life is unfolding in your specific manner to make you conscious.

The path before you often needs to be clarified. It would help if you cleaned off the cobwebs and debris from the last lifetimes. When you feel despair, remember you are drinking poison that your lower self* is dishing out.

Realize the beauty of your life. Focus on something other than your shortcomings or missed opportunities. Instead, think about the possibilities you hold in your hand right now. Reap your delicious gifts by harmonizing your inner world with the abundance around you.

Make this moment your friend, do not resist it. Instead, embrace it, no matter what it holds.

When you are present, there is no time. Time only exists in your memory or your anticipation. This moment happens now, and your life unfolds from Moment to Moment.

"A man sees in the World what he carries in his heart."
Goethe

Make Presence Your Destination

~

"When the goal cannot be reached, do not adjust the goal; adjust your steps." Confucius

We have many daily destinations in our life. For example, we go from home to work; this is our destination in the morning. The restaurant becomes our destination when we go out for dinner. Driving to a park, our hotel, our parent's house— all these places are our destinations.

What would happen if we made the drive, the walk, and the bus ride to our destination? The destination of Being Present while we are on the way. You can only be present at your destination if you are present en route.

. . .

We all have experienced inner turmoil when hurrying to arrive on time for an appointment, concert, play, meeting, or family gathering and not be late. Do you remember the last time you rushed through traffic, cursing your fellow drivers because they were not driving fast enough? Do you remember the last time you stood at a bus stop, fuming and ready to punch the schedule display because the bus was not coming? Do you remember walking briskly on a sidewalk, pushing and shoving through people to make it on time?

We all are doing this. We become like machines whose sole aim is to make it on time without considering the danger and havoc we are causing. Our brain switches off, and the maniac takes over.

I remember the first time I became aware of this madness many years ago while in Berlin. There was a meeting I had set up for another prospective student who wanted to learn about Peter Ouspensky and the "Fourth Way".

I was running late, so I drove tremendously fast down the wide boulevards in Berlin, not caring about the other cars, stop signs, or pedestrians. And then, finally, I ran a red light, and the camera flash brought me back to my senses.

The funny thing was, by the time I finally arrived at the apartment, the person did not show up, and the meeting was canceled—all this identification* for nothing. An expensive lesson for me not to get lost in imaginary requirements; a red-light ticket is costly, and yet no money is worth this experience.

· · ·

How can I listen to music at a concert when I am rushing and puffing to get there? How can I talk about my aim not to express negative emotions when I see people as obstacles that need to be shoved away so I can make it in time to an unimportant event?

How can I laugh with my family at the dinner table when I was, minutes earlier, ready to kill somebody because he did not drive fast enough?

When you finally reach your Divine destination, you find that you have never traveled at all! Instead, it was a journey from Here to Here.

These experiences are necessary for our Awakening. We must let them into our sanctuary so that they can transform themselves into Conscience. Conscience is the emotional side of Consciousness. It grows with our ability to Be in the Moment. It is our guide to the appropriate action and correct behavior. Conscience has nothing to do with culture, tradition, morals, or habits but is our emotional guide to stir us towards love, acceptance, and Godly behavior.

I often ask myself what Robert Burton would do when I am unclear. I sit in front of his photograph and ask for guidance to find the right approach, the best solution to a problem that needs solving, not only in a practical way but deep down spiritually.

Taking this Moment and reflecting on different solutions, I found his answer:

"Make the Divine Presence your destination. When you are present, the answer comes swiftly and directly. Be here now. Nothing is more beautiful and more rewarding than this Moment. When you are here, you have found the answer already." Robert Burton

It is typical of the *lower self** to set foot repeatedly in the same spot. You are repeating the same mistakes again and again. Awakening is about being aware of the error and not doing it again. Who can say they learned from their first mistake?

This learning is my work until I die. Remember, this life is only a transition for us; Paradise is in our grasp. Never, ever believe you cannot reach it now. If the rewards of your virtues and efforts are restricted to this present life, you are engaged in a contest where no prizes are ever offered.

Remember that to love is to be Present, and your Soul unites itself with God through virtues. Be aware of the fading of any excitement in your work. Be steady, be clear. Then, with your hands upon your heart, with extreme difficulty and great repentance, you can achieve the power and the kingdom.

. . .

Just be aware of your breathing right now. Make it your goal at this Moment. Words do not mean anything; it is your effort that counts. Make it an exercise to always be aware of your breathing, and you will walk the walks of the masters. This alone will produce Spiritual Consciousness in you. Lose yourself to find yourself. Be quiet, and become like God, whose language is stillness.

What is the true purpose of your life? It is not the worldly achievements; all the materialistic things life claims are unimportant. It is this Moment alone. Now and here forever, small and insignificant, but existing eternally.

The real purpose of us humans is to awaken, finding the Spiritual Consciousness that exists outside within you. Awakening is a journey where the aim is to reach the divine Presence. All else is pretense, the outer form of a human being's life that needs to align with this inner calling.

Aligning does not mean having a particular job, like being an artist or a successful businesswoman, but doing each job with intention, care, and excellence.

George Gurdjieff once said, *"I can only teach a man when he understands to make one thing perfect, like brewing a cup of coffee."*

It is not what you do but how you do it, not with vanity or showing off, but with the dedication of doing it right to please the God within you.

Refrain from being identified with what you are doing. Instead, find the space within, where excellence exists, the area where conscious actions are possible: beyond consideration, above judgment, beneath likes and dislikes.

"With the eye of my Soul, I saw the Light that never changes. I saw something quite different from any light we know on Earth. All who know this Light know Eternity."
St. Augustine

Transforming Suffering

~

*"A wise man, recognizing that the world is but an illusion,
does not act as if it were real, so he escapes the suffering."*
Buddha

From a worldly viewpoint, the desire for suffering and the transformation of suffering is the most incomprehensible aspect for somebody trying to develop spiritually. The capacity to embrace suffering and transform it is essential to inner growth. Suffering is inevitable in human life. The acceptance and transcending of this pain are the game changers in Awakening. Accepting the reality of suffering creates merit and makes one God-like.

. . .

Eternity is God's time within us. Therefore, temporary suffering and sacrifice are acceptable to us. We do not suffer; we prepare for the time when suffering ends. Only when we understand that suffering serves a purpose it becomes useful for us. When situations are difficult, our first reaction is to become negative. Instead, we must try to be in the Moment to transform our negativity and accept the friction.

The suffering we usually experience is unnecessary. We focus on imaginary problems and allow fear and worry to enter our minds and hearts. We create scenarios where we will be miserable and in pain.

Do not allow your mind to wander into these dark fields. Instead, try to see the thoughts and emotions of what they are: a decoy of the *lower self** to take you away from the beauty of this Moment. Unhappiness lies in unnecessary suffering, which is when we often extend these resentments into long hours and even days. Sometimes we are hooked to the poison in our minds, but to escape, we must create habits that take us away from these senseless occurrences.

One habit of transforming these imaginary forms of suffering is to create voluntary discomfort. For example, turn the heat off although it is cold in your apartment, sit in a slightly uncomfortable position, play some music you do not like, or skip the coffee you usually need so desperately in the morning. These little artificial pressures will bring you back to the Moment. They also help you create a will that prevents unnecessary suffering from disturbing your inner peace.

.   .   .

When you suffer, think about how you can approach the situation differently than somebody who does not know about Awakening. What can you do differently in this situation? Human beings enjoy smooth sailing through life, and disturbance is considered harmful. Sleep needs the avoidance of pain, so if you wish to awaken, you need the transformation of pain to create your *Higher Self*.

A Story of Pain

I clearly remember days when I could transform suffering for extended periods. For example, one day, while getting up from my sofa in my apartment on the 4th floor in Berlin, I felt an excruciating pain in my lower back. I fell to the floor and was instantly overcome by tremendous pain. My back seemed as if on fire. I felt the blood pulsating through my veins as tears rolled down my eyes, and I knew something was wrong. I couldn't move; every little movement sent firebombs through my body. My legs went stiff, my whole body contorted, and I lay still for the next few hours.

Finally, night came, but trying to reach my bed seemed impossible. I couldn't even get up to fetch a blanket or a cushion. I could only lay still and did so through the night. Some moments of sleep overcame me, but most of the night, I was left lying, moaning on the floor, getting colder by the hour, but without any strength to do something about it. Then, finally, morning came, and I rolled - gathering all my strength while trying to ignore the piercing pain - off the floor and crawled toward the kitchen. I hoisted myself up to make some coffee, and after a long period of slow, intentional movements, I could brew a cup.

My body suffered the next few days; every little movement needed immense strength and mind power. But being incapacitated and having to perform minor tasks in languid movements, I was present in my life. I saw myself crawling along the floor, sensing every part of my body, and hoisting myself up to rest on the bed. Making coffee or slicing a piece of bread became an intentional undertaking with Awareness involved in every movement.

After a few days, the pain subsided, and I went shopping. Walking down the stairs from my 4th-floor apartment took me half an hour. Holding the railing firmly and intentionally, gently placing every step not to cause too much pain, I felt like an old man. As I walked very carefully down the street to the nearby supermarket, I was awake to all impressions around me.

The slow motions of my movements became a movie where everything was in focus; I saw my feet on the pavement slowly moving forward, was aware of my arms hanging limp on my sides, the spring air felt fresh and soothing against my face, the laughter of children, the noise of automobiles, the pity looks from people, the wind.

I was present while suffering, or better, I suffered; therefore, I was present. Pain becomes the incubator for Higher States*, the instigator to Be, and the cause of Awareness.

My Awareness faded as the pain began withdrawing after the next few days. I did not wish for the pain to return but cherished the moments that helped me be more alive.

Transformation of suffering is one of the pillars of Awakening. Suffering is the ancient law of love. There is no quest without pain; there is no lover who is not also a martyr.

· · ·

Suffering is profound; friction is minuscule. We stroke our frictions like little pets of whom we are not afraid. We enjoy them. It feels good to talk about our little difficulties, the pain in the leg, the water not running hot enough, or the flowers in the garden not blossoming as beautifully as last year. Frictions are an easy trap for allowing ourselves not to accept what is given to us and to complain because life is not perfect.

You understand that we need to stop this bickering to continue on our spiritual path. It is not suitable to try to achieve Nirvana and then be disturbed by minor difficulties. Friction creates heat, which is necessary to forge our Being into Existence.

Real suffering is a mountain of pain. To lose one's job, a leg, or a loved one is a real pain. However, suffering is subjective and often an ego tool to find an identity. I remember suffering deeply, although all my external life circumstances were beautiful. I lived three blocks away from the beach, money was not scarce, and I was healthy. But deep inside, intense suffering was building up. The despair about my inability to quit drinking. My failure of not being present in my life. I felt lost emotionally and spiritually by not creating any more aims and exercises for my Awakening. This situation was suffering for me, although from an outside view, I lived a happy and satisfying life.

Everybody suffers. It is part of our life as humans. When you try to wake up, you need to transform suffering into

Presence. For somebody on the spiritual path, transforming suffering is a payment. Usually, people waste their suffering by lamenting loudly, going into self-pity, or cursing the Gods for allowing this suffering to happen.

For us Seekers, suffering and friction are a doorway to another part of ourselves. Hell is always there for our benefit. By transforming suffering, we become who we are. We can create beautiful Moments of Presence by submitting our emotions in silence. But this takes courage.

Early in our lives, we learned that suffering is terrible and something to avoid. But the hell we experience has brought us to who we are today. Friction and suffering are designed to keep us on course. So, we need to find the place in us to accept it.

Rainer Maria Rilke said:

"Why did I not kneel more gracefully to receive you?"

He talked about being in the Moment and not resenting what is happening. Acceptance leads to Gratitude. Here I am, thankful for the harmful shock of pain given to me. I wish to be shaken until I am shaken no more.

We can only be healed from suffering when we experience it to the fullest. But these attitudes require Being and require maturity in our spiritual way. The transformation of suffering is the most challenging task in our lives.

The German writer and poet Johann von Goethe expressed it as follows:

> *"One does not know in this case (when a close one has passed away) if it is better to release oneself naturally to the pain or should one, through the help which culture offers, transform and pull oneself together. If one chooses for oneself the latter, as I have always done, one is, for the Moment, in a better position. However, I have noticed that nature, through other crises, always breaks through and claims its rights."*

The transformation of suffering rips at the core of a human being. Suffering was given to us when we were expelled from Paradise. Reentering Paradise only happens when we transform our grief for a higher purpose. There was and is so much suffering in the life of human beings. Realize that you have been given the key to ending suffering by experiencing it fully.

"Remember, Denying Forces are Opportunities." Robert Burton

Negative Emotions

~

"Hearing one word of the Dharma makes one at peace."
Buddha

Negative emotions are poison to our bodies. They drain our energy, let us lose our equilibrium, and keep us asleep.

Positive emotions have a positive effect on our bodies. We relate them to a happy and fulfilling life. People, though, do not understand that many of our so-called positive emotions are generated from the lower self* and already carry the negativity within. For example, love from the ego is instead possessiveness and can become hatred on a dime.

The false personality is always unhappy. It needs to feed on negativity, anger, and fear. We need not listen to these thoughts but find peace in stillness and remembrance. This place of sanity is where you always wanted to be. It is not a Samadhi of a saint, or a temple or church, but deep inside your heart where love resides and present lives.

When you start to be fed up with your negativity and identification, you have begun the journey toward Awakening. The suffering in seeing your resentment and being unable to stop it is necessary on this journey. To experience the dealings of your lower self* is an essential realization for Spiritual Consciousness.

As you acknowledge your negative thoughts, do not be despaired. It is good; a light in your inner darkness has been illuminated. You begin to know yourself. The most significant revelation in this knowing is finding out who you really are and lifting the veil of ignorance.

Our ego, the false personality in us, fortifies itself with the identity of "I." It controls the imaginary concept of being somebody, of being important.

The philosopher and Conscious Being Peter Ouspensky once wrote that we would have to invent negative emotions if they did not already exist. A strange idea but quite correct in my own understanding. Negative emotions are necessary energy that can be used to create your Soul. By transforming negative emotions, we can redirect this energy into something higher, converting it into our Awakening.

The key to transforming negative emotions is to recognize them before they appear. Imagine one of these days when you roll over on the "wrong side of the bed." The rain is a gloomy hindrance, the bus is overcrowded, and your colleagues are a nuisance. On a day like this, you could be ahead of the beginning of these negative emotions by observing yourself and realizing that any occurrence today will create negative feelings. Do that by replacing these mechanical thoughts with positive ones. Be intentional and introduce new elements in the fight. Be thankful and grateful for this day. Your health is still vibrant, and your step is still young. Give yourself a little gift to lighten your gloom. Give a smile to a stranger to spread some love. Eat some ice cream, splurge on an item you have denied yourself for too long.

Remember that this day is your perfect training ground for the non-expression of negative emotions and the ability to transform them into something positive and rewarding.

You see the dark cloud darkening your beautiful sky, but you know it will fade away. Think positive, and you will look in amazement at how quickly your atmosphere can change. Be in the Moment; look at something real that creates happiness and joy. Your cat or dog moving at your feet, asking you for food and attention. Be here in this Moment. See it for what it is and let go of all the negativity that clouds your Being. Do not let these hostile forces drown you in oblivion. The sun shines, the world turns, and you exist still.

This separation from your negative thoughts is your transformation and catapults you into a Higher State*. It means you have introduced scale and relativity into your life. You have sacrificed something not real for something genuine: your aim to awaken. We change into reality when we let the aspects go that are not real. This happens when we recognize that we do not need to respond. We grow when we let go of expressing anger, discomfort, or resentment.

Making these changes shows you clearly the path ahead of you. The simple steps leading you toward the non-expression of negative emotions will bring you closer to your aim. Then, through a thousand mistakes, you are born. When you understand the trials, you realize the lessons are to give up your illusions and imaginary ideas about yourself.

Avoid, above all, self-pity. You have a God within you and Angels helping you to evolve. Your inner sun is shining bright, having started on the path of traveling souls. Therefore, do not allow yourself to be consumed by your lower parts. Instead, be uplifted and transformed through accepting suffering and the understanding that friction creates the necessary heat to be molded in God's image.

Remember that when you are negative about somebody, it is even worse when you are right!

We cannot change our life, but we can change our emotional responses. Remember, difficulties are opportunities. Try to see events from the perspective of a larger and more detached lens; this is an attempt to induce deliberate revelation. Everything is transitory. Refusing to judge brings incredible conscious freedom.

. . .

The legions of my negative emotions still hunt me today. I try not to be antagonistic against other people, but the thoughts return like a never-ending tape of misunderstandings and wrong attitudes.

I pray daily for the Gods to allow me to let go of these emotions, but they are repeating themselves, tormenting me with even more vital force. The love and acceptance expressed in Walt Whitman's writings and his care for other men and women are dear to me, yet not achievable.

Or maybe they are by seeing myself falling prey to these treacherous feelings. I am destined to grow into the understanding that everything is good and necessary. The strong wish to let go gets stronger. I know now that this is Awakening.

I sometimes ask what is wrong with me in despair, and the answer is always the same: Nothing. Seeing oneself is the beginning of Awakening. Realizing the power of negative thoughts and resentments in one's life is crucial to knowing oneself. When the negative emotions disappear, I am still here. Nothing has changed; they were a fleeting sickness of the heart and mind attacking me without conquering me.

This understanding is where Awakening starts. *"To Know Thyself"* is not an elusive concept about one's likes and dislikes. Instead, it is the truth about oneself. When you start to know yourself, you Be yourself. It becomes the reality of who one is. This task to know oneself is liberating. First, I must see myself and give up all the imaginary pictures and opinions. I do not have to pretend anymore. I need to see and remove the aspects unsuitable for Awakening. Being free of the illusions and lies that have governed my life so far leads to freedom.

. . .

If you wish to find the truth, avoid being negative and control your anger - the simple concept of Awakening. Be willing to relinquish negative emotions. It is a significant step in your inner work to realize that negative emotions are not part of your *Higher Self**; they belong to your *lower self**. The ego finds its reality and identity in hate, envy, resentment, and judgment. *It* does not want to let them go; they are a way of controlling us and ensuring that we are held down in the prison of our sleep.

The non-expression of negative emotions is not a suppression but a transformation. For example, imagine you are a military recruit, and your superior officer is yelling at you. You keep still. You swallow your negative emotions of hate because you know you will be reprimanded even more if you say something. This experience has nothing to do with the transformation of negative emotions. Your animalistic mind tells you that if you respond to the insults, it will be even worse. The transformation of negative emotions is the understanding that they hurt you and that keeping negative emotions in your heart is drinking the poisonous cup of sleep.

Realize that negative emotions are not real. Imagine what would make an Angel negative?

Could it be a bus being late on schedule, a traffic jam, or coffee spilling on your shirt? If you'd like to become an Angel, act like one. Once you do, you will grow into the role with time and effort. Imagine being better than you are, faking it, and then becoming it. You know it works in life; it also works for Awakening. Create the habit of positivity in your life. Nothing can deviate you from your aim to awaken.

The non-expression of negative emotions is, in fact, the control of our passions. I know you love your passions, the heated discussions about your political belief, and the preference for specific musical styles or movies. What does it matter? Do your likes and dislikes change anything in this world? Is your opinion worth anything?

No, it is the trap of believing something is real when it is just an imaginary idea of the world and its subjective perceptions.

A beautiful thought from Robert Burton comes to my mind:

"The last thing the lower self* will give up is hate; the last thing your Soul will give up is love."

We are fascinated by human beings that are able to love unconditionally. It is our ideal. So, be it; live it, try it. What do you have to lose besides your chains of sleep? So, let's walk this path together. Our most significant foes are within. You know it. I know it, and this is an excellent starting point.

Keeping accounts with other people is another burden that slows us down. I still have accounts with people from twenty-plus years ago that have long vanished from my life. But they still haunt me; they poison my heart. Letting them go is crucial for moving on. Do you want to drag out a lawsuit for years and years, being exposed to the negativity of its existence, to win a few dollars, to win satisfaction, to gain justice?

When you restrain your anger, you outrage the devil because you have tamed your animal self and subdued it. Keeping accounts is a well-known method of the ego to deny Presence.

It will help if you let go of your thoughts of resentment and anger to allow your Higher Self* to appear. Otherwise, your heart is blocked, with no room to breathe and no ability to walk above the clouds.

Circumstances produce no negative emotions. However, our *false personality* generates negative accounts and feeds on them continuously. Wake up to the reality of Awakening.

If you are negative, you are asleep. If you are angry, you are falling off your spiritual path. Realize that nothing can take away your equilibrium; it is impossible to knock you off your feet if you stand firm in love.

So be it, say it, believe it. Hell means the energy of acting on your impulses; Heaven is the energy of obeying something higher. Accept this motivational force and realize your power to let go.

To start Awakening, cast out all your troubles; it was just in your imagination. Let go of your self-importance. This earth is a speck in the universe; your place is invisible to the

Absolute. Therefore, do not think you have any privileged position.

Because you are nobody, you can be somebody.

"Holding on to anger is like grasping a hot coal with the intent of throwing it at someone else; you are the one who gets burned." Buddha

I am Real when I Am Present

~

"What you pursue is right here." Horace

My life unfolded in strange ways, bringing me, with every experience, closer to my destiny of Awakening. Spiritual Consciousness is not a fancy term, but the reality of my life.

It is simple to reach; no books and libraries need to be consulted, and no special skills or achievements need to be recorded.

It is to Be in this Moment, to experience the Now, the Presence. Unfortunately, we have been blinded by this simple realization with walls of philosophical theories and modern temptations.

With Awakening comes Responsibility. The meaning of our lives is not what we are doing but how we are doing it. Our lives exist in Being. It is not something you do but rather who you are.

Did Mother Teresa become conscious? Her efforts and dedication to the poor in Calcutta have transformed many lives. But it was an external action. It could only exist because people were hungry and sick. What would happen if people were not more ill and poor? There are no slums in Heaven. You might find my viewpoint insulting, but I bring it up because not what we are doing matters but who we are and from which place in us the actions stem.

Life only exists when we are. "I am" are the most essential words anybody can ever pronounce in her life. I am; therefore, I exist. Unfortunately, this shows René Descartes's philosophy got it all wrong. The thinking does not make a woman, but only the Being. The meaning in our life cannot be outside of ourselves.

Anything outside is primarily an act of the ego. Therefore, do not look at anything outside yourself; only the inside matters.

Part of looking outside of yourself includes traveling the world, a trap many people fall into. It was a fascination I, too, fell into for many years. Seeing different countries and cultures does make one more mechanically aware and present. However, I realized these foreign and beautiful experiences were a veil to keep me asleep.

It is a sour pill to swallow. I am not saying that you shouldn't travel on your way to Consciousness anymore, but you must understand that the new, unknown, and exotic is just a mechanical reaction without effort and will seldom lead to real change.

Somebody asked Socrates about a traveler who did not change after returning after years of being in foreign countries. Socrates replied that this is no wonder because he took himself on his voyage.

Spiritual Consciousness is to see your world at home new every day. I look at my garden and see little flowers appearing, others fading away. I see the light changing from early morning to midday. I take a walk and see the hummingbird feeding on the sugar water. Seeing my wife and her beauty strikes me, making me happy with the need to kiss her. So, I kiss her, and she chuckles, and I let her go to her chores, helping her and making her laugh with a bit of commentary about her beautiful smile.

I wake up early and notice the light changing, depending on the season. I grind my coffee beans carefully and pour the boiling water over them with intention and presence. I wait for the aroma to unfold and pour myself a cup of the precious liquid I long for in the morning. I read a poem. I write down a thought, and I hear my wife lightly snoring.

I am Present on this uneventful morning, one of many that make my life worth it. The morning might be the last one I will experience. I do not know, but it makes me even more aware.

I do some Yoga poses and thank the Gods for their care and love toward me.

And then sometimes a dark cloud comes over me: how do I pay for the inevitable car repair? I know money is tight, and I must learn how to handle the bills this month. I stare at my body in the mirror and see a belly forming, and my flesh is starting to sag.

Then I free myself from this misery. I realized that my lower self* was dominant again in putting me down, losing myself in the day-to-day challenges we call human life.

So, I choose to appear; I am more present. I shave and brush my teeth with the awareness of a God. I spray perfume on my body. I dress and look in the mirror at my appearance, understanding that what I see and like will soon disappear, a short story in the book of the world. I know that I am not unique. I am trying to wring out as many present Moments in my life as possible.

And is this what you always wanted for me? Is this the end of suffering and the beginning of my new life? I do not know. How can I? I live like anybody else, sometimes happy, content, sad, and pitiful.

How can I tell you about the richness of this life? I have tried many things. I went far and away, took everything they said would alter my mind, sang, danced, prayed, and made love.

Making love comes closest to my state of Spiritual Consciousness. Making love to a woman I love is lovely, but it still holds me as a prisoner to my desires and earthly bounds.

I need to make love to myself. Make love with my eyes seeing the lush clouds in the sky being pushed into different shapes by the wind. I love seeing the flowers in my garden and my walk in the park with the fountains and ornaments. There is so much we can be present to in our life. But, unfortunately, the more we have, the more confused we become.

I would love to be wealthy, but it does not matter for my Awakening. It is a minuscule aspect of the wonder I call my life. Do not be concerned with the little things in life. Life fools us by believing in its deceiving lies and bondage.

You can do anything and live your dream but do not identify with your achievements. Thank Higher Forces* when life pleases you but thank them also when they deny it. They know what it takes to make you Conscious. Understand the workings for your Being to appear.

There was a time in my life when life was financially rich. I imported Modern Classic furniture from Italy to Miami, FL, and sold them to design lovers around the US. It was not an easy job, repacking furniture from the containers shipped to me from Italy to Miami, but it was worth it. I was on top of my game. I was shutting down my phone at 5 p.m., lying on the beach, and not thinking anymore about the people ordering the next day. What vanity! What a deception!

I made good money, enjoyed life, lived two blocks from the beach, and thought this life would never end.

But the Gods taught me a lesson when I did not expect it. I suddenly fell into depression, started to drink again, and lost my business due to a change in the Copyright laws in the US, resulting in threats from enforcing lawyers representing the large manufacturers.

In addition, a more significant force was choking me by bringing the financial crisis to the US, rendering my professional efforts and new ideas to continue worthless.

Therefore, awareness is the power of the Present Moment. Your Spiritual Consciousness can slash the "Gordon Knot." Your real identity lies in bringing this power into the world. This happens now.

To start, negate the illusion of ego. The light of Consciousness is your Being that sees this entanglement, sees the craziness of the ego, and replaces it with Being Present.

Your identity lies in this Moment. I am that I am.

Behind the ego lies fear. The fear of being nobody, the fear of death. The ego always tries to cover this fear with specific achievements: power and money.

What becomes aware of your *lower self** is who you are: your *Higher Self**. Recognizing what is not real in you is already the beginning of what is real. The ego must feel superior, so judgment and resentment are favorite elements in its identity. A false personality gives itself moral superiority to other people. Gossiping is an element of this aspect, by revealing damaging facts about other people.

The ego plays roles in life to support its assumed identity. It thrives on recognition, praise, and success. However, for some people, fear is predominant, so the false personality takes the role of being insecure and hiding away. This is a sign of a lower self* that has taken the negative form of being inadequate and not good.

Confusion is a *Higher State** when you let go of the need to know. When you understand that you do not need to know, the unknown becomes a place of peace and clarity. The ego needs to be in control. But letting this control go allows your true identity to appear.

Observe your roles in social situations, seeing them change depending on the person you are communicating with. You are Legion. When you start seeing the different roles or personalities you are playing, you create a space where your authentic Self can emerge.

"Every day, we should hear at least one little song, read one good poem, see one exquisite picture, and, if possible, speak a few sensible words." Johann Wolfgang von Goethe

Acceptance

~

"I resist anything better than my own diversity." Walt Whitman

Acceptance is the pill the sly man takes to create his Presence.

Walt Whitman is teaching me the most crucial lesson of Awakening: look, observe, and cherish the Moment. Make it your own.

The Presence is all that matters, whatever it brings. May it be your life, destiny, and a lesson. You see your life's path unfolding consciously, finding your stance to exist. When you accept, you are grateful.

Embrace the opposites in yourself, and accept your shortcomings, fear, vanity, and lies. Understand that we all contradict ourselves. Observe, do not judge, and be thankful you finally see your reality. The veil of sleep lifts from your face!

Walt Whitman tells us:

"Whoever you are! Claim your own at any hazard."

We are in the perfect storm of our Awakening. Claim your place, secure your seat, and do not let them push you off with promises of wealth and fame. See it for what it is: a short moment in your life that can take you only down the abyss of Dante's inferno, suffering the idle beliefs that separate you from your own God within.

As you are, that is enough! I wish the Moment not to be other than it is. The Gods have destined us to awaken. Do not fight them; accept their way, and surrender to the wisdom of *Higher Forces**.

Now we are starting to see things as they are. Pure and simple. Our wisdom lies in our ability to turn circumstances into opportunities.

Face your temptations without squinting; look with both eyes and use them to your advantage. Then, wash your impurities off with the soap of acceptance.

Your false personality is fighting until the end. The negative thoughts will never stop, and the devils will always prick you with poisonous fruits. Spiritual Consciousness is not a function. Your ego will always call your experiences insignificant and deprive you of their value.

And that is the way you will suffer. Yet, it is necessary,

and you will be tested repeatedly. Everybody suffers, but we Seekers need to transform our suffering with acceptance and love and allow it to occur without the cries of "Why me?!"; "How can this happen to me?".

The answer lies in your Awakening. It appears in the awareness of your suffering. It reveals itself with the ultimate reward of your efforts, your ability to choose Presence over suffering. Our time is counted. There must always be friction to produce a conscious state in you. Endure it because it is the payment.

As you go along this path, always create the right attitude towards events in your life. Difficult circumstances do not happen because you're mistaken or flawed. They happen to put fire below your feet so that you can forge your *Higher Self** out of the suffering. Draw from the pain and transform it so that you may evolve.

This task is the most difficult one we face in our Awakening. How often have I beaten my chest to ask for lesser pain? How many tears have I shed with self-pity? And yet, I believe in the power of my suffering; I always try to accept it and not complain about it.

Consequently, I am saying these words without shame or hesitance. Accept your life. Accepting your faults, mistakes, anger, and fear will free you. Then you can be Present.

"Happiness can exist only in acceptance." George Orwell

Empower Yourself

"There is nothing either good or bad, but thinking makes it so." William Shakespeare

We all try to impress our friends, colleagues, and strangers. But our Soul is not looking to impress or amaze anybody. It is invisible, in love with itself, still and aware.

Rather than impress, go and love someone exactly as they are. And then watch how quickly they transform into the most excellent, authentic version of themselves. When one feels seen and appreciated, one is instantly empowered.

It is not easy to escape the demands of society, the awareness of being nicely dressed, the sensual look of somebody checking you out, the nod of approval, the glance of admiration. But do you want to be kept in the prison of vanity and fame? Do you want to please somebody and not please your Soul? Would you rather be flashy than calm within yourself?

You are walking firmly on the Road for 'Traveling Souls' when you feel lost in moments you are displaying vanity. You will be devastated by seeing your fascination with the empty symbols of sleeping life. You must understand that nothing is as essential in life as your Soul's Presence. You accomplish your mission when you create a permanent desire to Be Present. The Moment of your Awakening comes closer when you refuse all the riches in the world for your gift to awaken.

In this case, responsibility is excellence. You are doing the right thing even if nobody sees you. The trap of your assumed behaviors under the eyes of others has faded away, and what remains is your inner determination to be free, to do a good deed, and to become inspired.

Living our life this way is a constant struggle. Be inconspicuously present. Do not try to be somebody. Just Be; the Presence in you speaks the language of the Angels— accept it and allow the circus to end. The more conscious you become, the less you will take space. The fools are loud and try to impress. However, you impress me with your silence, kindness, and invisibility.

I love you for your soft and gentle way of leading your life. I am silent too. The words only mean something if you are in the correct state of mind. I want to remind you about this. I want to quietly whisper the answer you have long searched for in your ear. Be!

The little spark you ignited has burst into a flame - the flame of your Being that will devour resentment and fear. There is no failure when your Being is on the way. So do not wait for anything or anyone anymore. You have found the cure.

Our emotions aren't caused by what happens to us but by our interpretations of these events. Now is the time to give up your self-pity and gloominess. You have been chosen to be a God in your own right; Presence is starting to flow inside you.

How can you be angry or upset with yourself? How is it possible that seeing a hummingbird does not make you happy?

It is with all of us Seekers that we swing back and forth. This moment we connect to something higher, and the next moment draws us into the abyss of resentment and despair.

Do not worry about these things. They are happening along the way. Living through these episodes of being way under is part of our payment. The lower self* sometimes has the upper hand; it is strong, strengthened by many years of negativity. Be aware of your initial achievements. They are a milestone in your Awakening, yet the way is long, rising, and getting more treacherous.

.   .   .

Did you think Awakening would be easy? Did you believe that bliss comes easily? The Saints that went before us suffered and endured tremendously. They prevailed because they kept steadfast in their understanding that there is the love of the Absolute above all.

Many of our habits need to be revised in supporting to Be Present. These habits are legion, and we all have them. Self-pity, greed, resentment, jealousy. You name them, and I see them too. And yet, it is not focusing on the shortcomings, not giving space to our faults, but looking up into the sun and realizing that you can rise above the clouds. Above the clouds, there is always the sun. So, we must break through the dark sky that keeps us bound to earthly measures.

Be the miracle you would like to see in this world. It is not about big things; it is about the small, minuscule things that break through the dark clouds. A smile, a moment of just being without doing, a look outside the window and seeing the first flowers appear, a walk in the garden with your beloved, holding hands and smelling roses together. Drinking a hot chocolate afterward and ensuring she gets the best piece of the pie you bought in the bakery downtown. Life is simple. Negativity is complicated. The presence will always remain in our grasp, so do not let the negative mindset of the ego tell you otherwise. You are not simply a victim; you are now the prince kissed free by the princess - your *Higher Self*.

"Kindness in words creates confidence. Kindness in thinking creates profoundness. Kindness in giving creates love." Lao Tzu

Consideration and Connectivity

≈

"We must be willing to let go of the life we have planned to find the life that is waiting for us." Oscar Wilde

Our spiritual work cannot be measured in months or years. Our Awakening is in time. Once we really start on the road for "Traveling Souls," we cannot go back. We cannot stop without great suffering. Once you experience your Soul, you will be miserable and pained to have abandoned it.

It is better not to have started experiencing your *Higher Self** and then to leave your inner work. So often, a "weak searcher" becomes impatient with his progress and disappointed by the results. He needs to understand that real change takes time. When we start on the way, we are like a flower that has broken through the soil and finds joy in the sun. Our Higher Self* appears miraculously without effort, and happiness fills our hearts. But then, we need to nourish ourselves with efforts and exercises, like how a flower needs to be watered. Otherwise, we dry up; the beauty was just a brief appearance.

Real work requires being consistent in our actions. We keep our spiritual emotionality alive by creating daily exercises and aims for our Awakening. There is always an opportunity to not express negativity or recognize imagination* and to be aware of our favorite topics we identify by.

At the beginning of our inner journey, everything is clear. We are experiencing a "Kairos Time" where everything is possible. It signifies a crossroad in our life where real change can happen; a time of abundance, limitlessness, and grace.

To be reliable is vital. If you say you will do something, do it. Excuses are not possible. Feel the pain of the many, often opposing thoughts; see the prison of your willfulness. How can the angels trust you with the big stuff if you cannot be charged with the little things? So do right in all conditions; do your best, and do not be hurt when circumstances are not working in your favor.

Conscience is the emotional aspect of Spiritual Consciousness. It is to be aware of our actions toward people and social interactions. We understand right and wrong, not from a moral viewpoint but from Spiritual Consciousness. Therefore, we are alert and incorruptible in

201

our quest to obtain the most favorable environment with our words and actions.

Our Conscience is active when we are sensitive to the people around us and wish to spread harmony and joy. But it takes will and unity to bring it forward. Conscience is the sweet voice of our Soul whispering and is independent of our culture, upbringing, or personal preferences. It takes us away from self-importance. It is to know what this Moment requires, what makes life sweet and beautiful.

Spiritual work like the one we discuss has existed over the centuries under different names. First, it was called the Worship and Belief for a long time. Then, in the last few centuries, it shifted toward the Work of Reason. Today our work can be called Consideration and Connectivity.

Connectivity is vital to the eternal spiritual necessity to consider other people. We need to connect with other people through mutual sincerity and truthfulness to find the significance of our interactions.

Consideration for others is an essential measure of any inner achievement. We need to learn to serve. We rise by being humble. We lift ourselves up by worshiping something higher in other people and bow to the possibility of their Awakening.

Consideration is done with honesty. However, it does not mean hurting the feelings of somebody although sometimes we must strike their ego to awaken their *Higher Self**.

We need to find the true meaning of life and the inner workings of all the influences that reach us. Freeing oneself from unnecessary laws and material cravings induces thankfulness in us.

The search for our Soul needs to start with the understanding that everything in our life is connected; everything that has appeared and will appear is to make us more conscious and lead us to the truth.

This has nothing to do with Religion. Fulfilling the daily chores in our life, discovering the inner sense in experiences, being humble and honest about our dealings, and seizing the Moment as the only reality of existence is being a God in the making.

Everybody has her own truth. The difficulty is that most people believe that their own truth is objective. You will start seeing more when you understand that your vision is limited. When you stop imposing your opinions on others, you will begin to hear the eternal whisper of "To Be."

How often do you think of being right while conversing with others? Are you right in your opinions, maybe 70% or even higher, regarding politics, world affairs, or spirituality? If so, you could be a wealthy man if you apply your right-eousness to the Stock Market with even just 51% of your "right opinions."

Another important aspect of our work is to help other people find their own harmony and truth. For everyone we will meet, we can be a teacher. Accept this position as your quest within your own inner search. You are finding the meaning of your life by helping others find their own. So many people feel that something higher exists in their hearts but cannot rise from the burden of material weight and inner bonding.

Removing our chains to shine the truth into other people's hearts allows us to find our Awakening because of the confidence and hope we give others. This purity is not a form of sympathy or sweetness. Instead, we push others upward by making them strong, not weak.

Sometimes teachers are like parents who scold their children before going out to play and laugh with them.

Remember that we are all the same. When we smile, someone will smile back. When we can smile while firm and robust, our scolding is perceived as a blessing. When we are angry and not realizing our anger, we will render evil instead of good. Our work needs to be pure, joyful, and embracing. Only then can we continue.

Sometimes, we need to be strong in our quest. If somebody wants to hold us back or ridicule our efforts, pointing out our mistakes instead of our achievements, we must say goodbye and move on. You must remember your aim not to indulge in pleasing others. Be alert all the time.

It took me a long time to understand what Awakening is. Being Present does not mean you will never experience any more anger or jealousy. You cannot ban negative emotions from your life. It does not work like this. The more you evolve, the shorter the timeframe for letting go becomes. Maybe it took you one day to forgive your spouse for a hurtful word. But now you can forgive her after one hour. Your aim then becomes the quest to forgive her after one minute next time. This is our progress; this is our Awakening.

Realize that your judgments of others are caused by negative emotions. For example, you see a colleague skipping a required task at work, and you call him lazy. Did you ever consider that this person might work a second job, or his wife is sick, and he needs to care for her and the children? Perhaps he is just tired?

We have to accept our friends' mistakes to be able to accept our own. See the shortcomings and faults in your loved ones because acceptance with humility is the highest form of happiness. Never go to sleep without cleaning yourself with forgiveness. If you cannot say it directly, say it within yourself. Remorse is the pain in love.

Being positive weaves the invisible threat to the heart of somebody else. People do not remember what you said, but they remember how you made them feel. Love cannot be collected; one has to spread it like confetti. To find true divinity, one must develop the wish to help others. By helping others, you help yourself.

"Self-respect knows no considerations." Mahatma Gandhi

Silence

~

"What is a man? A mortal god. What, then, is a god? An immortal man." Heraclitus

S peaking is the most challenging time for everybody when one wants to Be Present. We fall asleep, losing ourselves so quickly in words. When we observe instead, we see a strong *identification** right at the beginning of expressing our thoughts; we become the words and cannot keep something alive beyond the uttering.

I have tried many times before giving a presentation or a talk to feel my feet on the floor, see my hands holding the sheets of paper, and intentionally breathe while speaking. Yet, seconds pass, and all aims have vanished. I cannot feel my feet on the floor anymore, my hands are left without Awareness, and my breath is just occurring without any attention or ability to sense it.

In those moments, I am lost. I identify with my presentation and charming, competent, and assertive efforts.

Somebody who can Be Present while speaking reflects a human who has achieved the highest form of Awakening: being separated from oneself and allowing the *Higher Self**
to flow freely.

For now, do not say something; Be somebody. Words are cheap; observe the world as it is— Be Present without words. One of the essential aspects of Awakening is understanding that the answer is not words, but your Presence, your state of Awareness, connecting with your Soul.

Submit in silence—the much talk of the learned people disguises their emptiness. When you are Present, you are quiet. Words destroy this Moment. Do you need to name your God-like state? Do you need to find a term that describes this experience? Your *lower self** will try to speak, explain, and find reasons for this Moment. But that is when you have lost it.

Many people are afraid of silence. They need to fill the precious void with comments and opinions. "What a beautiful sunset," "Just a lovely sight," "This is so beautiful."

These comments destroy the Soul's appearance, the ability to Be Present. Do not ruin your Awakening with empty words. Instead, separate yourself from this prison, take a stance, and become free of all unnecessary considerations that keep you bound.

Presence does not like to talk about itself. It just wants to appear; it just wants to Be. Your Awakening unfolds along your efforts to speak a little less and softer. Realize the greatest secret in this world is To Be the words but not to speak them aloud.

Do not fear the silence as you begin your Awakening; it is the space where we can meet— you and me, here and now. Do not lose yourself in unnecessary talk; Presence is just here, unannounced, real.

Be the eternal Now; Be the words. Leave behind what holds you back. Do you still wait for something? Do you grow older still expecting miracles? They are here already; they lie within you, and your silence speaks about them.

"Think not so much of what you lack as of what you have."
Marcus Aurelius

Reflection

~

"The unexamined life is not worth living." Socrates

The power of appearances makes us wonder in confusion, changing our minds often about the same things and regretting our actions and choices. Shed the light of understanding and revelation as part of your spiritual guidance.

Reflective thinking is necessary to understand your life, choices, and what happened to you. It is a forgotten thinking style in our fast-paced society. As a result, people act and do instead of reflecting and understanding.

Awakening is only possible by examining one's life. Reflective thinking is going inside you and seeing who you are, what moves you, what upsets you, and what makes you happy.

We need to learn from our successes and mistakes. But, of course, you can make every mistake in your life. It is okay to make many mistakes, but you cannot repeat the same error.

Our time is short, so avoid repeating and repeating the same mistakes. Do not allow your mind to think that along the way, something will change. A standard definition of craziness states, *"Craziness is when people do the same thing repeatedly, expecting different results."*

Mentally relive past situations and gain understanding about their meaning and lessons. Reflection gives you perspective. It shows you the tasks you need to learn and the value of your personal experience. It will provide you with an appreciation for the good and bad things in your life and help you understand why these events were helpful and supportive for your inner path.

We all have intense experiences; some people become thrill seekers to experience this "high" repeatedly. Others who have survived a dramatic experience are frightened and cannot face any situation that might be a reminder. But if you reflect on your experiences, you can separate yourself from them. Look at them from a distance, do not identify with what happened, and be a third-party spectator as you analyze the situation that took place.

Emotional integrity and the ability to put experiences in perspective and evaluate them can only come from separating oneself from the emotional experience. Thinking in clear terms about the causes and stimuli will help you see why you like to relive this experience repeatedly or why you want to avoid something similar at all costs.

Do not become tied into an emotional knot. Slash the knots that hold you back and throw off the emotional baggage.

Likewise, evaluate the temptations of the sirens supporting your addictions, making you crave them constantly. Reflect and understand why they have such power over you. *"And you will know the truth, and the truth will set you free,"* as the Bible states.

We paid dearly for some of our experiences, and to profit truly from them, we must revisit them. That is why you should reflect on your decisions in the past, especially the snap decisions. Then you will learn to trust your judgment and ability to go with your intuition and realize the sudden realization of right or wrong.

To understand the "big picture," you must reflect on the small decisions and experiences that were part of creating your life. What have you done that helped you move further on the path of Awakening? What incidents held you back? What have you seen in yourself that made you aware of the Moment, or which impressions made you run away from it?

The patterns of your life will become more apparent to you. Do you always respond with particular behaviors and emotions to a given situation? Do you react the same way to a challenge as you did as a child? To evolve, analyze yourself, look at yourself, and understand that you have grown out of these childish reactions from the past. Realize and embrace your growth. Own your life, Be the woman or man you want to be. Act if you need to, so you can slowly but surely grow into your truth.

When you reflect on your experiences, you can make a good experience even better. Make it count and value it. So many processes inside of you can only take place in the dark. When you shed light on emotional responses, automatic behaviors, and reactions, you free yourself from the burden of your lower self* and gain access to more consciousness and awareness. Your experiences are the jewels of your life; to see the brilliant colors, you must stare at them repeatedly.

This approach is not backward thinking, nor is it reminiscing. On the contrary, your experiences, especially the insight gained by looking at them, are your toolkit to act and your acquired protections to shield you from misconceptions.

You can support your aim to reflect and understand your past experiences by setting specific times during your week for your reflective work. For example, take advantage of your Sunday morning. After waking up, use fifteen minutes to reflect on the past week and review your experiences with a distant look, extracting some lessons and realizations from them.

Or go on a walk in solitude. Remove yourself from any distractions and be with yourself alone. Give yourself time for the memories to come. Do not judge; do not blend out. Just observe and be in the Moment for the reflection to penetrate your inner Being.

"Life can only be understood backward, but it must be lived forwards." Søren Kierkegaard

Be Moderate

~

"In this world of trickery, stillness is what your soul wants."
Rumi

Our technique is not some ancient, arcane secret buried deep within lost monastic scrolls. Instead, it is accessible to you right now by accepting your limitations and seeing your mechanics.

Try to establish good habits, a good change in your life, and a positive attitude as you guide yourself through your day. It is the practice of gradual, continuous improvement.

Say to yourself, *"I can create awareness in my life, and I can do it step by step."*

Make that shift, do not hesitate, and transition to your new Self. Every day something will be different; every week, something will be better; and when a month becomes a year, incredible changes have been achieved.

We live in an age of quick fixes and instant gratification, but our Awakening is neither. It is slow. Determined improvement can seem pointlessly small and insignificant when taken alone. How many drops of water will one day make an ocean? Transform your life.

Moderation is an essential exercise for Awakening. People ask why to moderate their life. Understand that greed and indulgence are the poison of our *lower self** spreading the short illusion of happiness. But we all know how short-lived our indulgences are, ending in a stomach pain reliever or headache pills to lessen the hangover.

"Eating with moderation is a lifetime effort," says Robert Burton, and I know the truth of his words. Doing it, or at least preparing for it, is a life-long effort. I know that alcohol is mostly the culprit to help in forgetting, indulging, and waking up the following day regretting our actions and behaviors. Alcohol is poison, and no matter how the advertisement agencies try to disguise it, it is still poison. Do you remember your first sip of alcohol, the disgusting taste of it? Now they are inventing all kinds of flavors to disguise the taste of alcohol while whispering in your ear the excitement of being tipsy.

Why do you want to forget your beautiful life? Is the reality of this Moment not superior to any imagination?

Remember, the Sufis use the expression *"being drunk"* as a metaphor for Being Present, to be with God. Therefore, nothing is further away from this divine experience than being drunk with alcohol.

If you start giving up alcohol, you will step toward Awakening!

Prepare your house, your sanctuary, your temple.

I am not a Buddhist or Jain; I kill insects almost daily. But something does feel more and more disturbed by this act. I kill spiders, flies, and ants and start wishing them well along their journey of death and rebirth.

But along my conscious journey, I am feeling uneasy about killing any living creature. It is because my Conscience is coming alive. Where is this uneasiness situated? I know this to be my emotional part of Awakening, but I still deny that I am killing and taking lives. I sometimes think about the Hollywood movies with giant Aliens crushing humans like ants. I am an Alien in this way.

But I do have to clean my house. I must take away the spider webs and kill the culprits. Being Present and intentional would mean removing the spider webs and catching the spiders to transport them outside. But I have no time; other things are more important. But wait— is life not meaningful and comes before anything else?

Changing one's character is a challenging task. There's a lot of truth in the power of habit. When we do something repeatedly, our brains rewire themselves. It is impossible to be kind or learn not to kill bugs overnight. It takes small, gradual changes, awareness, and the beginning of Conscience.

I aim daily to do at least one good deed each day. I was not killing the fly. I was transporting the spider out of the house, filling up the hummingbird feeder, and watering a dry plant. One thing a day, how do I brag about this? Then another good act before going to bed; how can I accept my Being of doing two good things per day? But over time, I learn that my slow and gradual change of habits bears the fruit of real change. Someday I will efficiently and habitually do kind things. I will become kind.

This is how we will become more Present in our life. We will create the space to finally appear.

"If one oversteps the bounds of moderation, the greatest pleasures cease to please." Epictetus

Positive Mindsets

~

"The greatest decision of your life is that you can change your life by changing your mindset." Albert Schweitzer

Prudence

Your prudence involves a good judgment of your current life situation. Although acceptance is always the first and most important element in looking at our life, there are circumstances when change is required. Especially when you are exposed to constant negativity from partners, your job, or your social environment. Removing yourself from these circumstances might be the right action.

Nonetheless, it takes courage to make these changes. Your perspective changes when you make your Awakening the most crucial element. Understanding necessary and unnecessary suffering is acquired through trial and error.

Gain the virtue of recognizing good and evil and act under this foresight.

An essential element in gaining prudence is the development of Conscience, the emotional aspect of Spiritual Consciousness.

William Shakespeare let Henry VIII say, *"I know myself now, and I feel within me a peace above all earthly dignities, a still and quiet conscience."*

Conscience understands right and wrong, good and evil, by not considering morality or conformity but looking deep down in your heart. With Conscience, we recognize what is before us without judging or blaming. It takes strength to not give into social accordance with the shared beliefs people bestow upon you. Rather, dismiss the moral attitudes society is teaching us. Conscience grows with our ability to live and understand excellence regardless of its form.

Consider the words of the Blue Fairy to Pinocchio:

"Remember, Pinocchio, be a good boy; always let your conscience be your guide."

Patience

Infinite patience is required to do our work of Awakening. Impatience comes from the ego, which rushes us away from the present Moment. We need time and stillness to connect with our Souls. Distractions and identification are bombarding our *Higher Self**. Instead of rushing, take the time to see, experience, and just Be. We need the time to fortify our achievements to crystalize our Awakening. Patience becomes the moral virtue that enables us to bear hardship and suffering without sorrow or resentment. It is a bulwark against the poisonous arrows of anger. Patience is a source of joy, a primary means of strengthening the love for this world and reaching perfection. It accepts the trials as reflections of the will of *Higher Forces**, making them mean-ingful and precious.

Perseverance

Shakespeare reminds us that "sweet are the uses of adversity." We all come across hardship, opposition, and defeat, but to endure is divine.

Genius is eternal patience. Understanding that time is needed to sculpt our masterpiece helps us to persevere until it is complete.

Remember that perseverance and consistency are essential in our daily practice. We must endure the doubts that will come our way and remain in a state of grace until the end of our lives. Although you will fall from time to time, your trust in your inner God - your *Higher Self** - will enable you to rise again. To persevere requires your faith for the ability to awaken. Your verifications will strengthen your confi-dence that you can be more present. You become emotional about Awakening when you make an effort. Small positive habits will lead you towards your aim. Start with one thing, and your being will change over time. Soon you will become hungry for more, destined to be more awake because you tasted eternity.

To evolve, we need to sacrifice something for it. It is an offering on our temple, signifying that we are ready. Nothing is too significant or too trivial as a sacrifice. We are relinquishing some simple pleasures, like watching Netflix or drinking hot chocolate in the evening before bed. We give our favorite sweater to a friend or give every person who asks us for money one dollar without exception.

Live your life by following your beliefs. Write them down. Memorize them and judge your actions by these vows. These are the foundations on which you build your life and work.

Being Self-Contained

Do not fall into desolation, feeling separate from the Gods. Feelings of abandonment, loss of purpose, and despair are attacks from the ego. Try to Be Present in these moments of internal negativity and realize that your ego is fighting harder and harder the more you swim upstream in your spiritual evolution. First, recognize these feelings of sorrow as a distraction or temptation to drive you off course. That will cause them to lose their sting. Pain, loneliness, and despair are companions on your way; bear it with your understanding that friction is necessary for evolution.

The Gods have chosen you to evolve. Why you have been selected? Nobody knows. But, being chosen is your infinite luck. There is now a song in your heart, a love song that makes you hum all day; the beauty of your existence has emerged.

Find consolation in God's reality within yourself. Delight in the joy of being alive and present. The sweetness of your spirit and the firmness of your high pursuit brings you bliss. Rejoice that you have found your relationship with *Higher Forces**, that they have embraced and invited you to share their immortal gift. A mark of outstanding inner achievements is your ability to find happiness in minor circumstances.

Your mystic union, the supernatural state of Spiritual Consciousness, is marked by the profound awareness of the divine Presence in you. You have revealed the mystery.

Be Kind to Yourself

The Stoic philosopher Cleanthes was walking through Athens when he encountered a man berating himself because of some failure. Seeing how upset he was, Cleanthes –typically one to mind his own business – could not help but stop and kindly say, *"Remember, you're not talking to a bad man."*

Discipline isn't about beating yourself up. There's a firmness involved, for sure. But, ultimately, after a lifetime of studying Stoicism, this is how Seneca came to judge his growth:

"What progress have I made?" he wrote. *"I have begun to be a friend to myself."* It is an act of *self-discipline* to be kind to yourself. To be a good friend. To make yourself better.

To celebrate your progress, however small. That's what friends do.

> *"Even if you can only make a little progress, Theaetetus, you should cheer up."* Plato

Reflecting the Light

~

"Loveliest thing in my invisible landscape, you that made me more easily seen by angels, themselves invisible."
Rainer Maria Rilke

Your Awakening needs to accept your many personalities and strengthen the one that serves your aim. Our lives are full of different attitudes and contrary thoughts. This is a common fact for all humans, no matter what picture they present in public.

I wish to connect as many of my life's characteristics to a higher world and my spiritual lifestyle - but often, they are not. Is this bad? Do I value the wrong things?

No, diversity is part of my human existence; it cannot change and will not because even when we are conscious, we are still humans.

Your Soul exists beyond your body; it appears while all your other functions remain. This explains why many Conscious Beings have unrelated personalities to their *Higher States*.*

Spiritual Consciousness is not a function. It exists beyond the human world and is untouched by biased behaviors or inconsistencies.

So do not judge your contradictions, for they will exist even when you have reached a more conscious level. But nevertheless, it is essential to recognize them so their power can slowly fade. Seeing them is the first step to unity.

Yes, "Moments of Light," "Presence," "Angelic State," or whatever expression you choose is unrelated to our human existence. It will only manifest apart from our human functions.

We know the Moment is always beautiful, yet we still worry about petty human identifications, like money, relationships, or fame.

But there are simple remedies to lessen these distractions and the opposing thoughts life provides. Because we can only have one thought at a time, we can let go of negative thoughts and replace them with gratitude. We exchange ideas of jealousy and envy with good wishes for the other person and realize that everybody carries their own burden.

Have you ever imagined that the person you envied as he drove by in his convertible Sports-car was on his way to driving it into a wall? Have you ever thought about the impressive appearances of people secretly anguished by sleepless nights and medications?

Reflecting conscious light in this world is not a passive or automatic process. It appears within our attitudes and choices. Almost always, when we are in the Presence of a "Real Human Being" or in places where Art in the form of music, painting, or poetry is present, we can tap into the realm of our supportive thoughts and behavior.

This is because what we focus on expands. To create good habits that bring us forward on our path, we need time, effort, and daily practices to support them.

Then and only then can we come into a sudden light, a moment of Presence, an understanding, a taste of *Higher States** that fall upon us as the much-needed mana to soothe our longing.

Accepting opposites and not despairing by the sheer endlessness of unproductive thoughts allows us to receive the wonder that flows freely in this world. Perceive and reflect the light in your thoughts and actions.

Nothingness and Not Knowing

You are content to Be Present between affirmation and denial, belief and disbelief, judgment, and acceptance.

In this place, you understand that a human cannot know everything and that some things will stay hidden.

Besides all the questions, doubts, and uncertainties, only the experience remains to have touched the miraculous. When this occurs, you have found the key to the miracle of life and opened the secret door to eternal bliss.

This place of not knowing is not one of ignorance or limitation but rather a place of acceptance and joy without the illusion of needing to be sure. Everything you ever wanted is on the other side of sleep. When you are Present, you know everything necessary to understand. There you will hang peacefully suspended in the space of nothingness.

Your faith is the sum of your verification, and you have verified that you are a God within, a Conscious Being in its own right.

Your faith is a positive attitude; never doubt what you have experienced. You have recognized the quest since the beginning of time.

Sure, you are weak in some moments and may fall back into doubt and illusion, but soon again, your recognition will prevail.

Nothingness is your emotional state of the irrelevance of words and concepts, the contentment of simply to Be, and the absence of any wish or longing.

You have nothing to lose besides the chains that hold you down. Grief has disappeared, the sun has risen, and peace is upon you.

Thingness versus No Thingness. Form and possessions

have become so important to many people. They do not see that space. Nothing and Being is our natural home.

You are not the form; you are where form does not exist.

"My soul, you must be very grateful that you were found worthy of such great honor." Francesco Petrarca

Happiness

~

"A well-guarded mind brings happiness." Buddha

Awakening is Happiness. Real happiness takes effort. It happens in this Moment, free of any longing or desire. It is without any form. The future will never give you any happiness; salvation occurs now.

As Jesus Christ said, *"Heaven is right here amongst you."*

Be not sad to have forgotten yourself or expressed negativity. Instead, be happy to see this now and rejoice. See these events in lifetimes. Your Awakening awaits you. Instead of judging yourself, be happy because your happiness does not depend on external circumstances. If it is not within you, it does not exist.

One Moment we are sad, and then something happens, and we are happy. Do not allow your ego to throw you off. Do not allow your Being to be cast into the abyss because of some misfortune.

Our life mechanically unfolds. If our happiness depends on achieving our longing desires, we are doomed to the endless recurrence of joy and sadness. Happiness is an experience of the Present, no matter what the Present is.

"The present might not always be beautiful, but it is always beautiful to be present." Robert Burton

Our happiness is the result of virtuous actions in our life. An act of kindness, a moment of inner stillness, not reacting, offering a smile. To do what is in this Moment; just looking when looking, just eating when eating. The simplicity of being happy is remembering our life in this Moment.

We are told to strive for riches in life: a new car, a bigger apartment, and stylish clothes. Whatever it is, we know that the happiness of acquiring an object gives us only short moments of joy. Driving the new car around feels excellent the first day, promising the first week, and then becomes just the usual form of transportation the previous vehicle provided.

Happiness does not lie in the objects or even the people we meet. We say, "My wife, my dog, my house," and know that these are only temporary companions on our journey. Only happiness beyond the grave is eternal and unchanging. This happiness depends upon how we spend our life.

. . .

William Blake:
> *"He who binds to himself a joy*
> *Does the winged life destroy:*
> *But he who kisses the joy as it flies*
> *Lives in eternity's sunrise."*

Joy is not in things; it is in us. There is only one happiness in life: to love and be loved. When you fall in love with a simple Moment of Being Present, this Moment becomes your life, your destiny.

Unhappiness is a disease. Negativity is polluting our world. The joy of Being is the only happiness possible.

Unhappiness revolves around blame and defense and protecting something inside of you that is not real. The only way to diminish these automatic processes is to do nothing. Letting go of your immediate reactions gives you unknown strength, allowing you to attain the power of being free from the entanglement of the world's web. Be small, be humble, do not show off, and gain your actual value, the value of being alive without form or pretense.

Be still inside. Do not name or explain the things in your world. Instead, allow the empty space inside of you to expand. This space enables your Spiritual Consciousness to appear.

Notice how the humblest things bring us joy and happiness: a glance, a moment of recognition. The smell of a rose, the cat brushing your leg as it begs for treats, the husband showing off his strength, and the wife understanding it all. Form, possessions, or external achievements do not cause happiness. Stillness and presence bring inner joy and harmony with the simplicity of the Moment inside of us. Therefore, you have been destined to know about this happiness that does not know loss or defeat.

When you are Present, you understand.

"Thousands of candles can be lit from a single candle, and the life of the candle will not be shortened. Happiness never decreases by being shared." Buddha

Learn the Truth

~

"Life is a dream, and all that happens in life is a dream. Death alone drives away sleep and puts an end to dreaming. Oh! May we awaken before death overtakes us!"
Francesco Petrarca

Our Starting Point

"To unlearn is as difficult as to learn." Aristotle

We need a definite method to refine and practice "The Art of Being Here Now." Your efforts must be sharpened and tuned in by a technique supporting your awareness. I do not propose a specific method for you. However, it will appear when the time is right and you are ready. The starting point is understanding who we are and what we can become.

Therefore, to wake up and follow the path of Enlightenment, one must know where one stands and where one begins. No one can escape without outside help. We need the grace of the Gods. As Homer said, *"All Men are in need of the Gods."*

We also need the guidance of human beings who have escaped before us. Of course, we need to study them and anticipate their lessons, but overall, we need to be touched by them. Learning from them will allow you to lift the veil that prevents you from seeing the reality of your existence.

When we see glimpses of who we are, we sometimes become frightened about the unnecessary negative aspects of our existence. To be horrified is good; it is the start of our Awakening. Be tired of your same old reactions to the challenges in life. Realize that there is freedom in reacting differently. Do you need to be angry when somebody is yelling at you? Do you need to be upset when you make a mistake?

All this is learned human behavior. You need to relearn and reevaluate, which will lead you to become a God. Do not be a robot, reacting in the same old way ingrained in you from birth. Love the freedom to explore new avenues, a new way of dealing with the challenges presented. Our freedom lies in the ability not to react anymore in the known, old way but in choosing our liberty.

. . .

You might ask, "What can I do?" but this question is wrong, at least initially. A woman or a man cannot do; everything happens to her or him. Like when it rains, or the sun shines — it just happens.

We first need to observe ourselves. We need to see who we are and what lies we tell ourselves. Then, shine the light of Presence onto your life. Do not just react to circumstances; take a breath, consider, and do not respond.

I know this is often impossible in the heat of the Moment. We are swept away by the *identifications** in our life. Somebody yells at you, and your instinct makes you tense; flight or fight - the animal kingdom has appeared.

The first step is Self-Observation, being aware of one's actions, thoughts, and attitudes without judging oneself. Many processes within us can only keep us asleep because they happen in the dark. When we observe ourselves, we bring light to these processes and interrupt their automatic appearance. Next, we must become frightened and appalled by what we see. Are we ready to do something that brings us closer to reality?

And remember to embrace your feeling of being disgusted with yourself. Remember the moments of defeat, cherish your shortcomings, and enjoy your incongruences.

"I exist as I am; that is enough. If no other in the world is aware, I sit content. And if each and all be aware, I sit content." Walt Whitman

The Lower Self* - The Beast in Us

"Beauty begins the moment you decide to be yourself." Coco Chanel

Within us dwells the Divine and the beast. We have witnessed these adverse emotions: compassion, humility, modesty versus resentment, jealousy, and anger. Do not judge yourself for these different sides of you. They are all within us.

We all have this animal intelligence, the beast that will devour anybody who stands in our way, the part in us that cries "me, me, me!" but does not know that giving is receiving.

When we start to understand, we have a choice. We become responsible for our life. No more being lost, no more sad days, no more giving in to the darkness of our ego. Instead, we are shining the light of our existence and shouting the message of love and presence.

There's really only one urgent matter: Being Present in our life.

We must study, observe, and examine its hidden agenda to rise above the ego, the false personality. These are the names of the forces that keep us asleep, the elements separating us from the meaning of life.

When I was a beginner at Being Present, my teacher

called me a "smooth operator." Years later, I understood what he meant by this comment, and since then, I have shined the light on the darkness within me.

It is such a liberation not to obey the *lower self**; I have stepped away from the abyss of being mechanical, a puppet in human form.

Something finally shines through when you see the many thoughts and beliefs you attach to your identity. It is the gift of Awakening, the beginning of your Presence. A tiny flicker of your Soul appears, and the Third Eye becomes aware of itself.

Rumi said, *"Leave the madhouse."* You must return to the Present, the only sanity we can have.

Do you remember the last time you were upset and were ready to kill for your conviction? Once the rush passed, did you ask yourself how you could have stooped so low? You must learn to understand that the thoughts of our ego are paper tigers and have no lasting effect on who we are.

These negative emotions come from our false personality. We look at them for what they are and repeatedly observe that they will subside slowly but surely. And when they are gone, we are still here!

Shorten the time to recognize these paper tigers, keep them from blowing up in your face, and do not allow them any reality. Do not take your vicious, negative emotions personally; do not feel guilty about them. Instead, transform them into your presence, a state of

acceptance and thankfulness. You stopped your *lower self**
in its tracks.

Understand that when the ego's attacks get worse, you have
advanced. Think of it as if you are swimming up a stream.
The current becomes stronger as you swim upward. The
more friction and resistance you experience, the further you
have gone on your spiritual path. Your task of Being Present
in your life becomes more and more complex the further
you go. See it as your progress. Do not believe the whisper
of your *lower self**, telling you how you are failing. Instead,
look at these moments with your *Higher Self** and thank
the Gods for giving you this Moment of understanding.
There is always a way out of the misery of being caught in
the fangs of the ego.

***Be Now Here – Do not believe the 'I's – Drop this
identification.***

In the beginning, these words will seem hollow and a lie.
But by repeating them, some calm will set in as an element
of sanity appears. My words become more natural, and the
chain of negativity gets weaker.

Whatever works for you— do it! Recite the words that
feel closest to you, imagine yourself slashing the dragon of
your imagination, and realize that nothing can harm you
when you connect to this Moment of your life, the challenge of your Awakening, the lesson to be learned.

· · ·

Omar Khayyam, the Sufi Poet, speaks in his poem about lifting the veil:

> *"There was the door to which I found no Key; There was the veil through which I might not see: Some little talk of Thee and Me there was — and then no more of Thee and Me."*

The veil is our *identification** with people, achievements, and preferences. It is the addictive sleeping pill life has prescribed to keep us asleep, veiled from the purpose of life to reach God, the *Higher Self** within us.

We have a habit of identifying with our problems. They seem so significant to us, but we might recognize the little open space once we step away from them. How minuscule all this is, living on a tiny speck in this vast Universe. Did you ever look at the night sky and realize your position? Have you ever felt the nothingness of it all? We identify and lose all relativity about our life, existence, and meaning. Wake up! Realize the difference between presence and imagination.

To escape, you need first to realize that you are in prison. Then, recognize the specifics of your jail. The *lower self** made your prison appear lovely and essential with all the goods and ornaments attached to the dark walls. The splendor of this world is just a temptation of the ego, making you believe life's crazy values have meaning.

.   .   .

Do you know of a rich man dying? Do you know of a poor man dying? It is all the same. What remains is the Soul, the meaning of this life, the journey taken, the values achieved, and the lessons learned.

Discover who you are. Being present is quiet, not angry, and not impatient. Presence is humble; it just is.

Give up your fascination to be influential; give up your aim to be somebody - fame displaces our presence easily, and people's attention corrupts our stillness. Instead, be simple, enjoy whatever life gives you, and stay humble. Smile rather than laugh out loud. Confusion and haste will displace your Being. Presence does not know any hurry. Observe your *lower self** and learn its tricks. Focus on your *Higher Self** and defeat the beast in you by ignoring its emanations. Just Be Here Now.

> *"When you awake in the morning, think what a delicious treasure it is to be alive, to breathe, to think, to enjoy, to love."* Marcus Aurelius

The Four States of
Consciousness

~

*"A pleasant and happy life does not come from external
things; Man draws from within himself, as from a spring,
pleasure, and joy." Plutarch*

T he only certainty we possess is To Be in the
Present Moment. Our life happens only in the
moments we remember. Therefore, the ancient
techniques of "Self-Remembering" and "Dividing One's
Attention" are crucial for our inner development; for our
ability to Be Present. It starts with "Observing Oneself," like
being aware of the door we open with our hand, tasting a
bite of food, listening intently to a piece of music, or
smelling the fragrance of the rain after a heavy downpour.

Seeing the differences in our awareness level, we understand that esoteric schools have always spoken of four
distinctly different states of Consciousness.

. . .

However, regular people only experience two of these states: "Sleep" at night in bed and "Waking Sleep," which is when humans do all kinds of things but are unaware of themselves and their surroundings.

Our quest for Awakening is realizing there is more to life than "Sleep" and "Waking Sleep." It makes us remember that there is another awareness from our last lifetimes and our desperate wish to continue with these lessons.

We long for a higher state of Consciousness where we know who we are. Only then do we possess certain qualities that we imagine having all the time: "Unity," the "Will" to do, and the "Consciousness" to experience our actions in life.

Within this *Higher State**, men can become Gods, but some Gods became men. Jesus, Mohammed, Buddha, and Meher Baba were chosen to give humanity hope and excellence. In their instructions, we can only imagine the highest Awakening possible for men: love and acceptance, gratitude and humility. We can't speak about this state but keep it as the infinite goal to become God-like.

The First State of Consciousness: Sleeping at Night

While sleeping at night in bed, people are not aware of their actions, thoughts, and emotions. Experiences during the day sometimes culminate in dreams. Many unconscious processes happen while we sleep. Modern research has proven that sleep is vital for our machinery's function.

From memory building over cellular regeneration to shedding harmful toxins, many aspects are happening while we sleep. It is a crucial unconscious state to keep us healthy. While we sleep, we have no consciousness in us or about us. Therefore, our body's functions take place without any intentional doing.

The Second State of Consciousness: Waking Sleep

When people wake up in the morning, they usually enter a state of waking sleep. Especially in the morning, many people say they are on autopilot, just going through the motions a human being typically does. Brushing one's teeth, dressing, drinking coffee, driving to work, etc. People can do all kinds of things but are unaware of what they are doing or how they are doing them. They only experience their activity as something they must do without grasping their existence and perception of being alive. Being alive means being aware of the things around us and ourselves. This allows us to sense and know that we exist, full of life and gratitude. But only going through the motions of earthly existence is just a shallow experience of what is possible for a man. No wonder "waking in sleep" causes frustration, unhappiness, and boredom.

Did you ever sense your feet on the floor while walking? Did you open a door and feel the door handle in your hand? Have you experienced drinking coffee and seeing yourself lift the cup to your lips? Have you intentionally shifted your car into gear?

You might have in rare moments of your life. These

moments occur when something out of the ordinary happens in your life. Maybe you fell in love, or a beloved person suddenly died. These are moments when external events impact us profoundly and make us more aware of ourselves. But you cannot live with the money you find on the street.

When you ask a person if they are here now, nature plays a trick by making this person, for a moment, conscious, becoming aware of herself. It is like waking up instantly from the dreamlike state that usually engulfs humans. So, people believe then that they can be present if they want to but fall immediately back into their dreamlike states afterward.

The profound secret in this world is that humans are not Present, are Not Here Now. Only a few people even want to Be Present and realize that it takes effort to achieve this ability. You will try to escape only when you clearly understand what sleep is. Only then life begins, and the desire to take hold will cause a new identity to emerge: the essence of wanting to Be Present. Escape the madness of wandering between the past and the future, and Be Here Now - your only place of sanity.

People do not value what they already supposedly possess. They'd rather stay in their sleeping-waking state, wandering and imagining fantasy worlds.

Thinking about the past is an illusion of things that might have happened but typically have nothing to do with reality. We tend to beautify or horrify our history depending on the story we like to create about ourselves.

. . .

Often, people project their innermost fears into the future. Fear is real only in very few instances. In these situations, we are prepared through our instinctive upbringing from the early stages of humankind, by skills and functions still active from our cave dweller times.

Our waking sleep hinders us from seeing the world as it is. It will stop us from experiencing this beautiful Moment that contains all the world's wonders.

How to Work with Waking Sleep

Everything begins with observing oneself and studying oneself without the lenses of judgment and glorification. This will allow us to find the weak spot in the wall of our waking sleep, to find ourselves missing something, and then to realize oneself was missing. Waking up for moments at a time and understanding that one was asleep for minutes, hours, or days is the foundation for building our experience of the Here and Now.

Our life before a computer can show us constantly our waking sleep. Modern technology sucks us in so quickly, and we are all lost in looking at websites, being fascinated by images and the stories other people show and tell us online.

I do create exercises around my daily computer intake. For example, after fifteen minutes of staring at the screen, I get up from my office chair. I look at the screen with its borders and stop for a few minutes to observe my breath. I read a poem or a quote on my desk. We need simple things like such to break the identification with the illusion created by a multitude of pixels and data.

. . .

Going to the movies is another prime example of how life tries to put us to sleep. It entices us to identify with a story, with people, with images intentionally created to fascinate us with computerized pictures and effects.

We can work with waking sleep by creating awareness in our daily lives. We achieve this understanding with simple exercises that help us break our regular life's momentum and mechanics. Efforts, like not crossing our legs or keeping our hands on our knees while talking, might interrupt sleep occasionally. Not eating while standing or permanently using a plate or glass will be a stumbling block for our thoughtless, mechanical behaviors.

And one of the strongest motivations to escape this vegetative state is to detect when one is asleep or when others are asleep.

This topic reminds me of Esther. She was my soulmate. I was crazy in love, fascinated by her smile and movements. But one day, I saw her asleep. I saw a human being away and gone into the clouds, her eyes closed, sleeping the dream of non-existence. After this experience of seeing my beloved asleep, I knew that love is an imagination. I cherished a woman that did not exist. This experience has haunted me since then. Finally, I had to let her go. Doing so ripped out my heart, but I had to continue my path of Awakening. I eventually understood that this incident started the formation of my Conscience. And when these moments of Conscience became more extended, I stopped fearing them. I stopped seeing them as emotional pain but instead as an element of subtle joy, a foretaste of my future's clear Spiritual Consciousness.

. . .

Let me also mention a movie I recall from the 1970s that impacted me immensely. "They Live" was the story of a man who found an abandoned box of sunglasses. Putting one on, he saw that Aliens ruled the world.

The President, the decision makers, all those people were Aliens flashing messages secretly on TV, movie screens, and billboards for people to sleep, conform, behave, and obey.

A powerful movie, and because I knew the truth behind it, it was frightening to watch. To reach Higher States of Consciousness, one must understand that regular life is designed to keep us asleep. So put on the glasses of liberation and wake up. Be Present, Be alive, experience this moment, and cast away the efforts of these aliens making you sleep and obey.

Liberation starts when you want to experience your life and discover yourself. So often, this is a frightening and lonely experience, but it is the only way to break free of the chains that hold us captive.

The feeling of missing something or being lost is the beginning of waking up. You realize that one was unaware of oneself and one's surroundings. This understanding is my strongest motivation for not wanting to wake-sleep any longer. I long to experience reality as it is. To Be Here Now and to look up into the shining sun, leaving behind the dark clouds of my self-made dungeon.

The Third State of Consciousness: To Know Oneself

We have heard the call "To Know Oneself" through the centuries. Those who lived by this goal are known as the titans of philosophy and spiritual achievements. This is because they did not stop to "know themselves" but achieved to "Be themselves."

Lift the veil of your imagination and live intentionally, aware, and consciously. We do have glimpses of this Conscious State. These are the experiences we remember, the incidents in our life that have a lasting effect on us.

This Third State of Consciousness sometimes appears through violent and horrible experiences or unique beauty, joy, and love.

Growing up in Germany in the 1960s, I was often irritated by my relatives who would recall the horrors of World War II. I even befriended an older man who told me about his time as a soldier in the First World War and his experiences. One of the stories I remember clearly is about him lying in a forward observation trench just a few feet away from the French enemy soldiers. They did not attack each other, holding dear to life. Their task as an observation post was to just monitor the enemy.

People remember these experiences because the horror of war made them more aware and Present. They understood that life could vanish in an instant.

Often people describe car- or other accidents with strange perceptions of seeing everything happening in slow motion and remembering tiny details of color, smell, and shape.

On the other hand, we recall ecstatic moments of love and joy vividly throughout our life. They engrave themselves in our memory, and we cherish these precious encounters as feeling alive, happy, and content. The moment we meet our soulmate, watch the beauty of a sunset while holding the hand of our beloved, and hear our favorite song for the first time...

This is when Moments become eternal.

We can create remembrances intentionally without exceptional circumstances. The technique is to Be Present with what we are doing and have awareness simultaneously. It is called "Dividing One's Attention."

Dividing Attention is the separation of oneself from the subject or object we are interacting with. We remain separate from what we do, think, or feel— just observing it and ourself at the same time.

Do this while listening to somebody without formulating opinions simultaneously in your head. Hold a glass of water in your hand, feeling the weight, seeing the shape, and taking a sip, being aware of the taste. Open a door and see your hand on the knob, sensing your arm's touch and movements pushing it open.

The Third State of Consciousness can be grand or minuscule. Nevertheless, it opens the realm to our natural existence, to our ability to live our lives with all their beauty and wonders. The more we experience this Higher State, we long for its return. And then, we start to see and understand more, and our desire to Be grows.

The Fourth State of Consciousness: To Know the Universe

I can only talk a little about the highest state of Consciousness a man can achieve. I have rarely experienced it. When I did, it was a moment of eternal bliss. I remember one Moment of the Fourth State of Consciousness after walking for hours in the Himalayas to reach a remote temple. That was when I saw the beautiful stupas miles away, separated by a river I could not cross. I sat there and listened to the chants from the monks. How can they reach me from so many miles away? How can I be so much in love with everything in this world? These God-like experiences are rare in our lives, and we hold them dear for all our existence as the Moments we were closest to God and finally understood the Universe.

People call this Highest State of Consciousness Nirvana or Paradise. It is usually too far away from us. Still, always keep it as your Guiding Light, as the aim of your existence. It will be in your grasp one day.

"Man will not exert effort for what he imagines to possess already." Epictetus

Obstacles to Awakening

∾

"When I walk alone in a beautiful orchard if my thoughts have been wandering elsewhere, I bring them back to the walk, to the orchard, to the sweetness of this solitude, and myself." Michel de Montaigne

Imagination

A line from a song by Chet Baker comes to mind: "Imagination is so funny; it makes a rainy day sunny." Imagination is an obstacle to experiencing the moment - it is not creative imagination. I do not mean the artist imagining a painting or a poem to unfold. Creative imagination immerses oneself in heightened awareness like a Moment of Presence.

The imagination I am talking about is useless daydreaming. These are the unconnected thoughts that enter our minds, stealing us away from reality. People love to daydream; they escape into an unreal world that allows them to forget their troubles, responsibilities, and, more importantly, the reality of Being Here Now.

I remember my favorite forms of imagination: sitting at a train window, letting the countryside pass me by, imagining things in the past or the future, and feeling drowsy and content without any attention, aim, or purpose. This habit is the sleep that veils us, the easy-going existence without reality, the dreamer's dreams.

This kind of imagination comes easily; it is the normal state of man, happening without effort or direction. "The Machine," as we can call a sleeping human being, is on autopilot, doing all kinds of things but unaware of them. How often has it happened to you that you drove home and were surprised at arriving at your house without any intentional action? You were daydreaming behind the wheel, not intentionally aware of traffic lights, other cars, or even the streets you took. You were asleep. We must observe ourselves to understand how common this is. Imagination occupies our whole life with short, lucky moments of waking up due to external shocks.

But now, refrain from allowing yourself this kind of daydreaming that leads you nowhere. Be aware of your life.

How to Work with Imagination?

In all our inner work, we need to see and observe certain ineffective habits and obstacles for our evolution. Naturally, we will be frightened by what we see. But these moments bring us closer to the sad truth of regular life.

We will soon understand that this kind of daydreaming has no value to us. It is a vegetative state that happens without any effort. It can take us to places we imagine to satisfy our *lower self**, the ego in us.

Daydreams are imaginary events and experiences that may never occur. The dreams of a loser, being satisfied with fictional ideas, and not experiencing the reality of life.

Modern technology allows us to visit all kind of wondrous places and sites from our homes. But, for most people, this has taken away the need to see and explore these places for themselves, satisfied with an imaginary, virtual experience.

Because of technology, life is made up for us to sleep. It gives you the pleasure of making money, owning the latest iPhone, having a house, going on vacation, and yet what remains in your life? Are the meetings about the company's latest sales numbers or the number of subscribers important for your Soul? Today our prison is called money and fame, richness, and exclusivity. You buy into these dreams - I sometimes still buy into these dreams, but the reality of Awakening gets stronger and stronger.

My Awakening started in me decades ago when *Higher Forces** awakened me for the first time to give me the taste of love, presence, and understanding. I am carving this experience out amongst all the illusions of life and continue to awaken on my own. I invite you to join me. But how?

Observe your breath right now. Look at this book and your hand holding it. Look up to the sky and see the sun shining.

It starts here; it starts small; it begins with You. I know this road takes work. It is not what your friends and colleagues approve of you. But it is the only way to come home to your destination, the destination of Being Here Now.

The most vital force for me is not to be in imagination but the wish to experience reality in my life. Of course, sometimes this reality is unpleasant, but it is my life, and every second counts.

Identification

Identification is considered in business a critical attitude in achieving goals and perfecting specific skills. The opposite is true. When we identify, we see nothing else besides the object of our identification, losing relativity and scale in our life.

I clearly remember intense moments of identification. This topic forces me to retell the story of racing through a night in Berlin, Germany, to make it in time for a postponed meeting. I was so identified to arrive in time that I drove at a maddening speed, even running a red light with a camera installed. Unfortunately, the camera flash only awakened me for a second from this madness. I continued the race without caring for the lives of other drivers or pedestrians or at least the financial impact this traffic violation would have on my meager budget.

Identification is one of the major obstacles in our evolution. It gets us into fights with people about ideas to the point of hitting them, losing all our dignity and human kindness. In business, especially in our job, management loves to see us identified with our work tasks and expects us to stay extra hours. We are asked to forget about family and other activities that make a harmonious and balanced life.

Identification keeps us asleep. Nothing can exist besides the crazy focus we call falsely productive. Yet, we all know the wonderful feeling of waking up from a long stretch of identification and returning to this Moment's reality. The birds sing the sun shines again, and the smell of flowers comes through the open window.

Identification has no relativity, and how often have we wondered later why we defended or proposed an idea or concept so intensely that we later abandoned or thought it wrong?

Identification makes us like a wild boar, destroying everything around us, our relationships, our peace, and objects that we smash in our moments of insanity.

For starters, we need to see who we are. Observing ourselves removes the lies and falsehoods we have created about our lives. Realize who we are: a machine whose buttons can be easily pushed. This is the beginning of our quest to let go of the attachments that are eager to cling to us. We need to see the reality of our puppet life, bound by strings that make us jump, react, and explode whenever a particular string is pulled.

How to Work with Identification?

The method of Awakening is to see our situation. Start by questioning the thought patterns society wants us to believe in. These could be false values some people want to feed us as right and admirable. When you do the opposite life is expecting from you, when you start to disbelieve what you are told and are being sold as eternal facts, you begin to walk the path of Awakening.

To go against the stream of life is complicated. You will see how often you would rather conform with others to get their praise or not arouse any conspicuousness. Waking up is uncomfortable. You start to step out of shared beliefs and structures created to keep you bonded and asleep. Allow this painful emotion, try not to be concerned about what other people think of you, and learn that swimming against the tide is the only way to create the real person you want to be.

We are working with identification when we connect to the universe, to something higher than the little current moment. How can one be identified with the little things life throws our way when our aim is much bigger than the job, the traffic, the argument, or the weather?

Escaping identification happens in small, tiny steps. Small, uneventful exercises teach us about the power of identification. They show us that we can start with the little things by making a difference.

If you want to eat this dessert right now, desperate for the sweet bite, do an exercise by waiting for five minutes before you devour it.

In a conversation where your passionate arguments are filling your head, do not express them. Let them go and listen. Avoid exceeding the speed limit if you are driving late to an appointment.

. . .

Because our life is filled with identification, every moment is a chance to break the chain that keeps us bonded. Break the chain by simply letting go for a few seconds, a few minutes. This is the time for your eternity.

The Many Thoughts (no Unity)

Man has no Unity. We consist of many thoughts, personalities, and attitudes that have nothing to do with each other and often are controversial. I refer to them as the many "I-s," constantly attaching the word "I" to them but meaning only a fraction of my entity. Experience this separation in yourself, the pain of opposing thoughts and emotions.

Look at Tarot Card Number Ten, The Wheel of Fortune, displaying a wheel with three monkeys. The top monkey carries a crown and scepter, representing the Monkey King at a moment in time.

We are the same. We say "I," but this "I" comes only from a small part of ourselves, a fleeting thought, a hasty promise, a whim of the moment, but the whole woman must pay for it. Think about how often you promised to keep something secret, to keep an aim, to follow an exercise, to love your wife or husband until death, and how easily all that was broken. It was forgotten, put aside, or neglected because the "I" only ruled for a moment without the rest of the other elements of your being and personality knowing or approving it.

We have no Unity, and the lack hinders us from completing our aims and aspirations and, in return, shortens our promises. It allows us to do the opposite of what we said moments ago.

How To Work with Not Having Unity?

The significant obstacle to our inner evolution is to be many, but not the One. For example, today, you want to do something; you are passionate about an idea or concept, but tomorrow you do not remember your aim anymore or have forgotten your convictions and inner belief. I have changed from being a socialist to a conservative; I have switched from proposing free love to finding the one love worth pursuing. Such decisions are not age-related only. It is acquiring different understandings caused by experiences that make us question our convictions. Opinions mean nothing; a man needs a firm attitude to become honest and robust. Whatever your aim is, make it beautiful and good.

Life is beautiful; your fellow men are here to teach you and make you understand your challenges. Accept them to be different and walk your path of Awakening.

Observing is always the key to understanding our situation. First, we need to see who we are. Then, we must get fed up with our faltering aims, shallow aspirations, and flip-flopping.

At the same time, we need not judge ourselves. Instead, our understanding grows when we see the reality of human life. We need to be grateful for being allowed to see this. Everybody is legion.

Negative Emotions

Expressing negative emotions is our primary obstacle on the path of Awakening. It is the big trap we fall into constantly. Not only blatant negative expressions like anger, rage, shouting, or quieter forms like jealousy, envy, mistrust, judgment, and ill will, but also inward-pointing aspects like fear, hopelessness, boredom, and self-depreciation are our constant foes.

But remember: negative emotions are not real. They express our *lower self**, destroying our efforts "To Be."

If a woman only works with the non-expression of negative emotions in any form in life, she is on the sure path to becoming conscious.

Negative Emotions also manifest in our postures and body language. It is the most potent weapon of our ego to destroy any possibility of Being in the Moment.

Often negativity against other people can last for a lifetime. This leads to the inability to forgive an insult or hurtful encounter for years and the loss of friends and family by allowing the false personality to keep a grudge, feed on judgment, and devour any possibility of forgiveness.

For all of us, working on negative emotions is the most crucial aspect of Awakening. Lessening their hold on us is necessary for spiritual evolution to take place.

Even the kindest person you meet in life does have negative emotions. They might not show them publicly, but nobody, not even a Conscious Being, is exempt from being free of this enemy.

. . .

How to Work with Negative Emotions?

To stop expressing negative emotions is an almost impossible task. No matter how much we mentally prepare ourselves, negative emotions are too fast to be blocked by intellectual attitudes.

It comes down to the timeframe for letting go of our negative emotions. By working on ourselves and creating positive attitudes in life, like thankfulness and humbleness, we can shorten the timescale of the negative emotions holding us hostage.

It took you an hour to let go of your anger when fighting with your spouse, and now you can forgive after ten minutes. Letting go quicker is real progress; one day, you can reduce the timeframe to ten seconds.

Many enlightened masters observed that our breathing changes when negative emotions boil up. Therefore, when meditating, we learn to observe our breath, to sense our breath coming in and going out. We calm down our minds by keeping our breath as normal as possible. Noticing a change in our breathing signifies that negativity is starting to arrive. Hence, to be able to observe these changes helps us to separate from them, and that is real progress.

Epictetus, a Greek Stoic, suggested preparing for situations where we know that we might encounter disturbance and react with negativity. For example, he advises us to mentally prepare before going to a public bath or swimming pool because people will shout there, splash water, and behave foolishly and uncontrolled. Knowing this beforehand, we can deflect our reactions to these events by anticipating what we will face.

"What wisdom can you find that is greater than kindness?" Jean-Jacque Rousseau

Understanding the Human Mechanics

~

"Don't curse the darkness; light a candle." Confucius

Our Four Brains

We, humans, are creations in the image of the Gods. We are gifted with grace from the first print of somebody's hand in the caves of Lascaux to the self-portraits of Rembrandt or the poems of Rumi.

We share these beautiful gifts of humanity not only by creating them but also by appreciating them. I remember a female friend's simple and powerful words: *"I am no longer sad that I never became a concert pianist. Instead, playing the piano is now part of beautifying my life and not being remorseful for missed opportunities."*

She had exchanged some imaginary ideas with the reality of her life.

Her words reminded me of the story of the two students talking about their teachers:

The first student was raving about the miracles his teacher can perform: "He writes on one scroll, and the words appear on another. He can recite all the scriptures by heart and be in two places simultaneously."
The second student just said: "My teacher's miracles are to walk when he walks, eat when he eats, and listen when he listens."

Finally, I have realized the simplicity of my life as a miraculous place to appear. A lifetime away from these foolish situations when I questioned my intellectual abilities as a pupil, wondered why I did not understand the blackboard equations, and asked why I was not selected for my town's best-players team to compete.

The philosophical statement of René Descartes, *"I think, therefore I am,"* is a decoy of mechanical life to make us believe in thoughts as a unique value. Are your thoughts worth anything? Are your deeds not more important than thinking about doing something?

Descartes cherished the human function that thinking is the same as to Be. To think is a start; to Be is the completion.

In other words, do not be fooled by your intellectual mind. Life has cherished this human function as superior to others. But is it so?

Let me explain the blueprint of our human machinery. It is what it is. No judgment, but seeing it gives one the freedom to understand reality, the meaning of life, and our destination.

In addition to our intellectual mind, we have three other brains that often overpower our Intellectual Brain due to their higher reaction speed and intensity of expression. Our thoughts, or phrases with the prefix "I," come from different and separate places in us.

Our **Intellectual Brain** is the center where we manifest with thought and reason. It is in our head and is concerned with thinking and storing information. As with all of our brains, there are different levels available to man, which differ in their ability of intentionality.

Some people's thinking is repeating simple concepts heard and learned from others. Other people are much more sophisticated and can think about a topic, connect different aspects, and bring forward ideas and concepts that benefit humanity. These people are the "Einsteins" of the world, the thinkers and philosophers whose ideas have shaped our world.

· · ·

Our **Instinctive Brain** is the center where we control and manifest our automatic functions, like breathing and blood circulation, but it also influences our senses and intuition. It is placed around our genitals, functions mostly automatically, and is concerned with our body's survival. It has preferences for specific foods and bodily sensations. It is very much worried about the safety and comfort of our physical life. Our so-called thoughts of being too cold or hot, comfortable or miserable, needing a drink or food come from this Brain. Depending on the person's ability to use the Instinctive Brain more intentionally, they can strengthen a healthy disposition and fine-tune their senses.

Our **Moving Brain** is near our Instinctive Brain, and both are interconnected. The Moving Brain is our intelligence that orients in space and directs our outward movements. It stimulates and controls the idea of working out, walking, or picking up a craft or hobby. The intentionality someone can bring to this Brain can be easily observed. Some people are excellent in sports, playing an instrument, or constructing elaborate models, while others seem clumsy and often described as having "two left hands."

Our **Emotional Brain** is connected to our heart and is concerned with all emotions and feelings about ourselves, others, and the world. Its wide range embraces feelings of cuteness, like those expressed for babies and puppies, to the more profound emotions of sacrifice and service as part of a broader purpose in life.

. . .

Understanding that negative emotions are not part of our Emotional Brain is essential. Instead, negative emotions are artificial and relate to all four brains. We begin seeing reality when we realize that negative emotions are not real. They are the bile of our *lower self**. Negativity appears in us often due to instinctive discomfort. For example, being hungry or too hot creates negative emotions in us. Our false personality makes us believe this negativity is justified by finding an outside culprit for one's misery.

We are only genuine when we let go of our negative emotions, transforming them into gratitude and thankfulness.

Suppose a woman or man is working only on not expressing negativity but transforming them into love and consideration. As a result, this person is destined to develop and reach the ultimate goal: to be free and walk with the angles in the Here and Now.

> "When I was five years old, my mother always said happiness is the key to life. When I went to school, they asked me what I wanted to be when I grew up. I wrote 'Happy.' They told me I didn't understand the assignment, but I told them They didn't understand life." John Lennon

Types of Human Beings

"Whatever purified your heart is the right path." Rumi

We are all different, and yet we are all the same. This is because we have been given a specific "machinery" in this lifetime. Therefore, our evolution depends on accepting what we have.

You are who you are because your life needs to unfold according to a cosmic plan. The Gods never fail. They want you to become conscious and be a Buddha in your understanding so that you may join them in Paradise. The Gods have chosen your parents, country, and socialization to bring you to the starting point of your journey or return to the milestone reached in your last lifetime.

Do not be afraid to see your life as the expression of external necessities to bring you into Being. Saintly people are

267

conscious because they understand life's circumstances are the stepping stones to evolution.

We always make a profit when we realize the gift we have received, the remembrance of our Soul, and the call to Be Present in our life as the stairway to Heaven.

Do you oppose the idea that there are different breeds of dogs? Do you deny the reality of the difference in appearance, size, attitude, and demeanor between a Bulldog and a Pincher?

This is the same with us humans. Some of us are German Shepherds; others are Labradors or Beagles. But who cares? We need to be concerned about our ability to cherish this Moment to accept who we are.

This common saying also applies to Awakening: *"It does not matter the size of the dog in the fight, but the size of the fight in the dog."* So, what is the size of the fight for Presence in you? Are you waking up in the morning thinking about how you can reap Presence today, or do you think about all the denying forces that could make this day miserable?

We have a choice in our life every day. If you failed today, pray in the evening to do better the next day. If you fail again, repent, and find some little exercises to help create Presence.

Would you criticize a baby for falling after taking a few steps when learning to walk? Why do you blame yourself for learning to walk? Applaud yourself for trying. Enjoy the first step, and be happy to have taken it, even if you fall after the third one.

Awakening is as simple as life. Be happy, be content with your current situation, and strive to improve. Love your struggle, embrace your mechanics, and realize you have been given the right circumstances to awake.

Acceptance is the pill the wise man swallows in any adverse situation. It is the saving grace for our evolution. What power do we have besides accepting the things happening to us, the way we are, the body we possess, and the thoughts we are thinking?

When we accept, everything fades away. To Be who one is, is the greatest secret in the journey to Awakening. The grass is never greener on the other side; it is just different. Enjoy your grass, your circumstances, and your set-up. It is designed by *Higher Forces**.

Categorizing humans into specific types is a classification of our outer shells, bodies, and earthly existence. It does not reach into our Soul or our evolution.

Understanding my mechanics as part of a specific type of human being is helpful. The secret is to accept oneself as one is: the inner meaning in explaining human types in astrology, the Enneagram, and other psychological tools. When we begin our journey to the Present, we need to start with what the Gods have given us: our body, our thoughts and feelings, our upbringing, and socialization.

And we ask, as I have often asked myself, why am I like this?

The answer becomes more straightforward as I continue my journey: "I am who I am. I accept it, do not reject anything, and be happy with what was given me."

We all have multitudes and are not limited by specific features.

Astrology is one way to show us that we differ according to the day, hour, minute, second we are born. At the beginning of my search for Presence, I was very interested in astrology and its ability to predict people's lives by their charts.

It can be a revelation to see the blueprint of one's life unfolding according to specific chart elements, the planets, signs, and houses. But astrology shows only the external path in one's life. It does not show our Being to deal with specific incidents in our life. Your Being, your ability to work with shocks and challenges, is not part of your chart; it is part of your efforts to create Being.

You have a choice in your life, whoever you are. Your choices are acceptance, forgiveness, not identifying with external events, and remembering your aim.

What is it that makes us who we are? Are you happy and content with what nature has designed for you? If you are poor, accept it or change it. If you are negative, see it and change it. Imagine the power of changing your life, being who you want to be, and emerging as the prince in the fairytale disguised as a frog.

Do not be afraid; you have nothing to lose besides your chains. If you fail, it will be at least a story to tell, but if you succeed, it will be a new world, a new existence, a life with meaning, destined for Paradise.

"Intelligent individuals learn from everything and everyone, average people from their experiences. The stupid already have all the answers." Socrates

Our Strengths and Weaknesses

~

"Being willing is not enough; we must do." Leonardo da Vinci

W e all have strengths and weaknesses; our task is to acknowledge our gifts and salute our blessings. Imagine your ability as a child to make up stories and tell your toys about your adventures and wonders of this day. But, of course, you believed everybody could do this - no big deal.

When I was a child, I could distinguish different smells. Different flowers in the vase had their specific odor. The morning after an early rain shower gave the air a particular scent, and the clothes of my school friends had all their distinctive emanations. I thought everybody could smell these things. Only later in life I realized that my heightened sense of smell was something special. The perfumes of some women made me cringe or cry with lust. The odors of people around me either ensued disgust or pleasure.

Now I understand my specialty. What is yours? Can you think about abstract concepts in your head? Do you feel somebody's emotions and are touched deep inside? Can you jump high and run fast like not many others? Do you draw or form sculptures out of nothing? Are you perceptive of moods and the energies around you?

Acknowledge your strength, focus on it, and develop it as your skill, profession, and sanctuary. After this, let go and realize that this gift is just part of your mechanics, your contribution to life. I promise you other gifts will be waiting for you here.

These abilities are mechanical. People make a big fuss about their skills to create perfumes, develop mind concepts or chemical formulas, or break a world record. Do not get me wrong; I especially admire the Olympians who constructed their life around running a second faster, jumping a centimeter higher, or lifting an extra pound. They have done what we want to do with Awakening.

If we can put the same focus on Awakening as they have done with their physical and mental skills, we will awaken in this lifetime. Can you? Will you? What hinders you from being the champion in the Olympics of Awakening?

I know the answer, and it is not easy to accept. Our "machine" wants to be better, faster, stronger, more beautiful, and more desirable. But these achievements are formulated through our ego as part of our mechanical life. Awakening is no contest. Nobody will congratulate you on it. Nobody will put you on a pedestal, shake your hand, or give you a medal. No, they will crucify you; they will tell you that you are wrong, that you are mistaken, that your life has gone off the wrong path.

They needed to crucify Christ to feel better about themselves. They needed to dispel Mohammed, refusing to listen to his sermons and accusing Buddha of adultery to find anything wrong with a Saint.

Are your friends asking you why you have become quieter? Less fun to be around than before? They tease you and ask what is wrong.

Yes, something is wrong with you. You have started to wake up, and going against the stream is causing friction.

Because of this, you may sometimes feel alone and abandoned, but it is the only way home. Home to your destination of Being Present. Home to being a Conscious Being seeing the world as it is. You understand your friends and family and know you must say goodbye to their identifications, joys, and expectations. Something else is waiting for you. I'll find you there.

"There is no path to happiness; happiness is the path."
Buddha

Elements of Change

~

Letting Go

"Be present at every breath. Do not let your attention wander for a single breath." Gujduvani

We need to understand the urgency of Being Present. But this depends on our lifetimes. So, we must go through a series of lives while bringing us closer to the culmination of our existence. Have I reached my final appearance on this planet Earth? I do not know, but there is no more doubt that I will awaken this lifetime or the next - it makes no difference.

. . .

Attention comes now more often to me. I can now do many things in my life with attention. I hear my voice speaking; I see my fingers on the keyboard typing; I take a sip from the glass; I look out of the window and see birds flying; I see tree branches moving in the wind. I am adding more and more attention to the simple moments of my life. Why is this so difficult at times? Why is the most beautiful thing in the world so hard to achieve?

It is hard because Awakening goes against all the mechanical streams in life that keep us bonded. Sleep is all around us. People do and act but are not aware of it. Only some realize our existence makes us building materials for the Angels to shape into form.

All this happens at this Moment. Observe yourself, feel your breath, look and see, and remain inside. This is the miracle of life.

Rumi knows our challenges:

> *"But strong hooks hold you in this wind. So many people love you; you mix with your surroundings' color, smell, and taste."*

We are like a fertile field in which all virtues grow abundantly. But weeds are growing there as well. It is our task to plug a thistle and plant a rose instead. We need to realize the blessings that have brought us to this Moment. Your understanding of these words separates you from the rest. Other people are content enjoying their dreams, never waking up to the reality of conscious life. As a result, Awakening is a lonely quest.

We would love to find understanding in others: we wish our friends to love us for our efforts. But no! We are alone in our effort to be more intentional and awake. We are not getting lost anymore in the lover's face; we are not laughing with our friends about just anything. To be here, to pay attention to this Moment, is a lonely endeavor. Those who have gone this way tell you about the splendors of their findings and the flowers on the road to Heaven, but you need to let go of your petty identifications now.

> *"Afoot and lighthearted I take to the open road, Healthy, free, the world before me... Henceforth I ask not good fortune; I am good fortune... Done with indoor complaints, libraries, querulous criticism, Strong and content, I travel the open road." Walt Whitman*

Feel your hand letting go. With gentleness and love, look at the friends who no longer understand you. They may not be aware that you have been called to see the wonders of this world. Still, embrace them and then let go. They will always be dear to you, but now you must go on to your destination of Being Present.

Come with me. The first step is to feel this book in your hand, the light hitting the page, the sounds outside your room, and the cushion on your back. I got you. You got me. Let's be here together.

The searcher will reach the point where he becomes utterly oblivious to this world. He is present at every breath. He does not let his attention wander for a single breath. He remembers himself always and everywhere. What a beautiful concept to awaken. Let's become the Olympians in our life to hold on to the beauty of our existence and be united with God.

Efforts

"Some men relinquish their designs when they have almost reached the goal, while others, on the contrary, obtain a victory by exerting, at the last moment, more vigorous efforts than before." Plutarch

Happiness is effort. The effort to Be Here Now never tires and never disappoints. We are making efforts in our life to be more present. It will make a difference. A beautiful inner state of peace and confidence comes afterward.

Make the efforts small and invisible. Only attempt a little. Aiming for something unattainable is a way for the *lower self** to break you, to show your incapability to achieve anything.

So start small. Start with reading a poem instead of the news. Start with brushing your teeth and feeling the handle of the toothbrush. Start with sitting down to drink your coffee and feeling your feet on the floor. Start with looking up while walking and see the sun shining upon you. Start with not expressing frustration because your commuter train is packed with people.

The ego knows how to crush us, and it knows our weakness, being the weakness itself. Continue because you must. You have tasted the "manna of heaven," your Presence. Now continue, do not let go. Try again and again.

Today your body feels weak and asks you for a break. Give it two minutes, and then continue. Do not indulge in the crankiness of your false personality. Instead, make this day beautiful by trying to Be Here. Nothing else counts.

Whenever I imagined I had reached the end of my abilities to make an effort, I heard my *Higher Self** whispering: *"This is the beginning."*

Awakening has come within my reach. The start of my new life of Being Present. The assurance that I am walking with God.

The more we understand what we are doing, the greater the results of our efforts. It is a spiritual principle that our achievements are proportional to our understanding of our work and the Consciousness we bring to it.

If you try to Be Present, greater demands will be made upon you. So continue to swim against the river of sleep. The further you get upwards, the stronger the stream becomes. Nothing will be forgiven easily if you have made efforts and sacrifices for your aim to awaken. You cannot lie to yourself anymore; you are now responsible for acting by your understanding.

Even a tiny offense against your understanding might wipe out years of effort and inner work. The more you awake, the more you become responsible for your actions.

When you observe something in yourself that you dislike, do not try to eliminate or destroy it. On the contrary, it will become stronger by giving this feature energy. Just observe it, bring light to this process, and you will see that it loses its grip and power over you.

When I demonstrated in my youth against wars, nuclear energy, apartheid in South Africa, or the endless exploitation of natural resources, I gave power to these horrible aspects of life. Give your energy instead to the beautiful elements in life. What you focus on expands. Along the way, you will eradicate the bad. To have virtues in life is self-defense - strong beliefs of excellence help keep oneself healthy. Spiritual efforts need a strict guarding of our thoughts.

Presence is outside of time and place. It is different than being good. To Be Present is to reach the thoughts of good and evil beyond human life. So, abandon the world and let it go. It will lead to a rewarding life.

You are what observes, not what you see. This understanding is the pinnacle of our efforts, the ultimate realization of what we want to achieve. Something is looking through your eyes; this is the real you.

"It is the charm that defeats death," as Epictetus pronounced. So, accept this state of your existence. Of

course, it takes courage, but what choice do you have now anyway?

All our little efforts are pointing toward a significant change. Invisible personal efforts seem like nothing, yet they mean everything because they comprise our lives. So now is always the time to make an effort.

Making an effort is not to climb a mountain externally but internally. We need to make rightly placed efforts. Then the Gods, Higher Forces*, or whoever you name this power will do their part. Accept it, even if you do not understand it now. You will when grief disappears. You will when the longing is gone.

You do not need more teaching; you need more effort. If you reach the top, keep climbing.

Aim

"Pursue worthy aims." Solon

What are your aims in life? How shall your life unfold, and how will it end? Decide whether you want to know, explore, and understand the eternal truth. There is no better pathway to self-realization and coming into Being than composing and conceiving the highest aim for your life. Commit to it!

Ask yourself if there is anything more inspiring to do than to fulfill your highest purpose, your god-like existence, and allow it to come into reality.

People aim to earn five more dollars an hour, work thirty-five hours instead of forty hours, or afford a vacation for the family once a year. Be aware of adopting similar aims. To do this, you must orient yourself.

Orient yourself daily and find the tools that work for you to live your aspirations and higher meaning. When you create your aim and formulate it without doubt or hesitance, the world will shift and support you. So, focus daily on this aim and organize your life around it. You will see unknown possibilities and receive help from unknown sources and new endeavors.

And yet, your focus will also bring new challenges and difficulties. You will be tested and pushed off the pathway—always get back on track and become unshakable again.

Your life will have gained meaning far beyond any fleeting wishes and aspirations. This meaning will bring you through the difficult times and keep you afloat despite the storms hammering at your door.

> *"Ask, and it shall be given to you; seek, and you shall find; knock, and it shall be opened unto you." (Matthew 7:7)*

Remember that setting your aim is a process. First, you formulate what you want, and then you will receive what you need. Please leave it to Higher Forces* to guide you. Look at the signs along the way. Adjust and continue. Set up your life according to your wants, look inside, and do not fool yourself.

Finally, be honest.

This thought brings a film by Andrey Tarkovsky to my mind about finding the truth and seeing the lies we tell ourselves.

"Stalker" is a guide that leads people through a dangerous zone, a wasteland devastated like the surroundings of the reactor zone in Chornobyl. He promises to bring them to a ruin where their inner wish will come true. But first, they must overcome many mind-boggling supernatural and dangerous situations, and in reaching this ruin, they understand that the wish they imagined was not their real inner wish.

Overcoming the obstacles to reaching this place has shown them what they truly desire. Not world peace, not to find a cure or end world hunger, but, in fact, petty wishes for richness, success, and personal fame.

This might be your story, too, that after trying to achieve your high aims of Spiritual Consciousness and Fulfillment, you realize that it was not your real inner wish. But this realization is also part of your journey. So, will you be ready to see the truth and know who you are? At the beginning of our path, we are clueless; we imagine and believe. It is a time of imaginary ideas and sentimental platitudes until the real work starts to emerge.

. . .

You understand that you need to make sacrifices for your aim. Imagine an Olympian athlete with the ambition to win a gold medal in his discipline.

Due to the long hours of practice, the body is aching with pain, the dietary restrictions, the denial of leisure time, the control, and the mental surety that she will be successful. You must bring the same commitment to your aim of Awakening; nothing less will do.

To start, look at yourself as a stranger. Observe who you are and discover what you can become. Start right now. Do something small so that you can achieve it. It makes you victorious and sets up for you the mind of a winner.

Your human desires and mechanical wishes will always try to get in the way because *the lower self** is destined to interfere. This is the real inner struggle, the friction that creates a presence in us. This is the only war worth fighting, the internal battle between good and evil, between waking up and sleeping.

We achieve our ultimate quest to Awaken with our daily life's small, inconspicuous aims. For example, daydreaming is the opposite of any beneficial mental activity. Therefore, focus on a specific purpose to stop daydreaming. This habit is hard to break, but remember, little by little, results will show.

That could be driving your car to work and keeping both hands on the steering wheel. Refuse the chance to daydream when taking the commuter train to work. Sit on the train and look up instead of down, consider the other people, and listen to the noises around you.

Find your aims and efforts. Whatever works for you,

but find something to break the momentum of daydreaming and being in imagination.

It always takes extra effort to accomplish aims. You previously heard about the law of octaves and the need to introduce a new force to achieve our dream. Everything happens in life to the rhythm of non-excellence. If you want to be different, then you need to act differently. Remember, the *ego* wants to make you believe you are tired and likes you to see that things are done when they are not. Awareness of these traps is the only way to complete and keep aims.

Nothing can be achieved accidentally; nothing has value without bringing conscious meaning. When you start to understand, you are beginning to break your chains of slavery. You begin to see how people live, what constitutes their aims of existence, the objects of their desire, and their life aspirations. And then you need not judge. Instead, it would help if you were thankful for being given an understanding of the meaning of life.

Formulate your aim in your quest for Awakening. Make it personal; make it tangible. No objective can be too small. Find the right place inside of you where love begins and never ends. I'll meet you there.

Attitude

"Like a wheel in perfect balance turning, I felt my will and desire impelled by the Love that moves the sun and the other stars." Dante Alighieri

The attitude to live a life of virtue is problematic because often, these attitudes lead one to become zealous, prideful, hypocritical, and filled with doctrine. Whatever we do is weighed against our aim to evolve. Do good deeds, but do not be proud of them. Do not strengthen your vanity by doing them; tell nobody. You do not need your name to appear on walls of charitable gifts.

Humility is a positive, brilliant, divine attribute. Forgiveness springs from humility. Judge not and be not judged; do not condemn and be not denounced.

Our attitude to these events is our only power when encountering difficulties and friction. Of course, life is often tricky; things do not go how we intended them to, but no matter what, we have the freedom not to react mechanically with frustration, anger, or disappointment.

The moments of separating from the shocks we receive are our actual achievements. The secret is to develop a dispassionate attitude.

There is a story of Epictetus, the stoic philosopher who was an enslaved person in Rome. His master was upset with him and tugged violently at his chains. Epictetus calmly told him that if he continued, his other leg would go lame, and his value as a slave would greatly diminish.

Once we realize the true nature of things, we can separate a little from the immediate emotional reactions that govern our lives. Creating the right attitude towards Awakening means cherishing nothing as crucial as our aim to awaken. Who or what can take this away? If I am not for myself, then who will be for me?

If we, for example, consider other people too much, if we feel the necessity of always pleasing other people, our attitude creates inner slavery and dependence. In the most common situation, we are identified by what others think about us and how they treat us. As a result, we experience this nagging perception that we are not appreciated enough. It is a constant leak of our precious energy. In difficult situations, do not react negatively when responding to an insult or critical comment, but ask a question instead: "Is this how you feel about me?" or "Did I do something that upset you?"

Clear the negativity away; nothing good can come out of it. Instead, replace it with a wish to understand and keep your inner balance.

Our sincerity depends on the attitude of seeing other people as our mirrors. We need to develop the mindset that nobody is our adversary, but everybody is our teacher. We always profit when we focus on learning rather than defending.

We must remember our true aspirations to recall the passions of our intimate moments. Create a beautiful attitude towards yourself, be your friend, connect with your life, and cherish every Moment.

. . .

We are constantly identified with what is given to us at this Moment. If it is nice, we are content and happy; if it is difficult, we are annoyed or angry. We are the puppet that reacts to whatever comes to us. We are Pinocchio, the puppet who can become a boy. It is time to cut our strings and act with Presence to become real.

Thankfulness

"A wise man never loses anything if he has himself."
Michel de Montaigne

Students on the path to Awakening take *Higher Forces** on their conscious terms daily. They use any occurrence to create Presence.

Be thankful for the revelation and inspiration you have received in your life. The fruitless knowledge so many people are proud of leads nowhere and provides only conformity.

Conformity to the will of the Universe is a virtue that brings inner peace. Trust and rely on the providence of the Gods. Be thankful for the gift bestowed on you. You have been chosen. Now act on this privilege.

I am sure you have loved somebody in your life. The woman or man that you thought would make you happy forever. But nothing outside of you will ever make you happy; it is within you, the grace bestowed upon you to be yourself, the master of your own life, and to see the beauty of the Universe.

I cannot tell you about these wonders of beauty; you must see them yourself. Your life has finally started, and you are giving up the lies of human life. Be thankful for these realizations. I know they are not easy to accept. Yet, you still think there is value in life.

So wake up! Be Here Now. No eye ever saw the sun without becoming sun-like; your Soul cannot see beauty without becoming beautiful. Therefore, be courageous enough to take the risks of accomplishing your God-like appearance in life.

And when the lower self* tries to defeat you, you will already know who you are not. So be the one you are, an evolving Soul Being Present in the life given to her. Be thankful for this understanding; it is the only thing that matters.

You Are Special

"As to me, I know of nothing else but miracles." Walt Whitman

A sperm faces incredible odds of uniting with an egg and forming a new human life. It is the story of all of us.

. . .

During sexual intercourse, about 300 million sperm enters the vagina. Afterward, millions of sperm will flow out of the vagina or die in its acidic environment. However, many sperm survive due to the protective elements in the surrounding fluid. Next, the sperm must pass through the cervix and open into the uterus. This opening is usually closed and opens only when the woman ovulates.

Once inside the cervix, the sperm swims toward the uterus. Millions will die trying to make it through. Inside the uterus, muscular contractions assist the sperm on their journey toward the egg. But many sperm here are also destroyed by the woman's immune system mistaking them for foreign invaders. So, half of the sperm swims toward the empty Fallopian tube and the other half toward the tube that contains the egg.

At this point, only a few thousand sperm remain. The tube has an outward current, and the sperm must surge against it. Some sperm get trapped here as well and die. By now, only a few dozen of the original 300 million sperm remain. The sperm must push through an outer layer surrounding the egg. The first sperm to encounter the egg will fertilize it.

With this information, how do you believe you are not special? Nature designed you to be the woman or man you are today. There are no chances; everything was created for you to appear.

I appeared. I rose consciously out of the abyss of self-pity, despair, and doubt and entered the bright sunlight of this miraculous world - the meaning of life, the beauty of our existence, the Here and Now.

Angels Helping Us

≈

"Time may come when men with angels may participate."
John Milton

Gautama, the Buddha, is quoted saying that there were many Conscious Beings before him and that many Conscious Beings will come after him.

To awaken is the heavenly aim for a human being to shed the burden of sleep and to appear fully developed. But there are degrees in the spiritual development of humans.

Few humans reach the most profound Consciousness and the ultimate God-like appearance. Jesus Christ, Mohammed, and Buddha, the three founders of the world's main religions, are completed human beings in this understanding.

Other conscious men and women are still developing

and must help other evolving souls ascend on their path. Like Dante's "Divine Comedy," where the author is guided by his mentor Virgil, we have angels around us who are teaching and helping those who have entered the Way. Walking on the Way for "Traveling Souls" means to have understood that Awakening is the true meaning of life, and nothing is more important than Being Present.

For us Seekers, this Credo is more than just words. We have a permanent desire to evolve and develop our *Higher Self**. Now, we have help from Paradise.

My guide is Walt Whitman, the poet of the Soul, and the Body, whose Spiritual Consciousness is expressed in his epic work, "Leaves of Grass."

You will meet your guide to your Awakening when you enter the Way. It might be the music of Johann Sebastian Bach that speaks to you, the self-portraits of Rembrandt van Rijn, the plays of William Shakespeare, or the verses of Sappho. You will find your guide when the time has come, and the light of your Presence helps you go firmly on your path.

This world is full of miracles, and Being Present in one's life means seeing these miracles. Is the sunset coloring the clouds in red velvet, not a blessing? Is the deep, amber smell of a rose, not a wonder? Is your ability to feel, sense, and kiss not a gift? Understand when you awake, everything is a miracle, and your guide will appear to accompany you on your inner journey.

Walt Whitman – The Soul Is Always Beautiful

"Through anger, losses, ambition, ignorance, ennui, what you are picking its way." Walt Whitman

When I visited my teacher, Robert Burton, in the Foothills of Northern California more frequently, I always stayed at my friend John Graham's house. I met John for the first time in Munich, Germany, around 1988, where I tried to establish myself as a PR Journalist in the Bavarian capital. He often visited me after his assignments as a "Gentle Moving Coach" in Europe. Until he died in 2010, he was a teacher of movements based on the famous "Alexander Technique," which he developed into his gentle and consciousness-awakening postures technique.

My apartment in Munich was the first time I heard Walt Whitman's poems. John had always carried his copy of "Leaves of Grass" with him and loved to read it out loud to me in the mornings in his low and warm voice.

Later in California, during my visits, our mornings on his sun-filled terrace became well-designed rituals of feasting on beauty, taste, and inspiration. Flavors of different jams, preserves, and sweets are still vivid in my memory, served on beautiful little plates, cups, and glasses he had collected on his journeys. Then, after we had filled our urge for taste, he'd just start to read some words from our friend Walt.

· · ·

Love flowed instantly at these beautiful lines, and my immediate reaction was the warmth of being content and happy in this Moment.

I became immersed in my reading of Walt Whitman. I discovered we were both born on the same day, May 31st.

Reading about Walt's life story, it didn't surprise me to see similar life attitudes and experiences by having both the Sun in Gemini at around ten degrees. For example, his aimlessness and job hopping related to my aimlessness as a youth. Likewise, Whitman's lack of social and economic success combined with high self-esteem was like my experiences in my twenties and thirties.

Although I do not know Whitman's chart, it is evident that the same sun position in Gemini would yield a similarity in the outward expression of our personalities. Information like this helps us to be less identified with our shortcomings and flaws, understanding that our make-up is just the stage for us coming into Being.

Whenever I read "Leaves of Grass," I am transformed by his views of the beauty of every woman and man. I am humbled by Walt's ability to love and admire anybody and anything on this beautiful earth. His pure love is without resentment, not the slightest critical thought, just the recognition that everything is beautiful and meant to be the way it is.

We know that this kind of ability can only be earned. We understand that it is formed under heated pressure and strengthened by the will to accept and endure.

Like all of us, Whitman has suffered from unreturned love. It is the fate of all lovers to suffer through the experience of rejection and dismissal. But he is using this experience effectively. He is using it for his own transformation. Everybody suffers in life. To see the merits in our suffering is the task for us Seekers. Accept it, embrace it, and then use it for being in the Moment, for being thankful that the sharp dagger has awoken you a little.

> *"Sometimes with the one I love, I fill myself with rage for fear I effuse unreturned love,*
>> *But now I think there is no unreturned love,*
>> *The pay is particular in one way or another,*
>> *I loved a specific person ardently, and my love was not returned,*
>> *Yet out of that, I have written these songs."*

When we see and observe something outside of our identifications, we realize that our view is corrupted mainly by our thoughts and premonitions of what we see. Therefore, seeing people and things – like Walt, without judging or adding anything- can only be achieved when the Soul is pure.

Just like Walt, I have walked the streets of Manhattan and Brooklyn. I have traveled far and walked many other streets filled with people, smells, and noises. I had only seen glimpses of the ability to see without judgment. But these moments were beautiful. In these moments of my Divine Presence, I felt this love and compassion; I sensed inside me the ability to accept and allow everything around me to penetrate and uplift me.

. . .

I clearly remember one afternoon in late October in Ahmedabad, India. Sun-rays were filtering through the heavy smog caused by cars, rickshas, and motorbikes, honking and making noises as if life depended on it. There was no chance to cross the streets, no traffic light to stop the flow. I was being pushed by the masses walking the sidewalks, flushed with the flow of bodies moving in one direction. The smell of spices and old, rancid cooking oil reached my nostrils and made me sick. Voices of people as a wave of sound pushed into my ears with force.

And yet, I was present in all of it; no negativity inside of me reached the place of seeing, smelling, or hearing. The unconscious touch of these people pushing against me was not answered by anger or distaste but rather by the sensation of being part of a big wave flowing down the streets. And I just let go and Be.

I saw my world that afternoon, as Walt describes in his writings. I could let go and Be in the Moment without judgment, opinions, preferences, or denial.

Even stranger things did happen to Walt and me during some years when my focus on Awakening became diluted. I was falling off the path of "Traveling Souls"; my *lower self** was running the show, and I felt helpless to change direction. As a result, I became inconsistent with my efforts, forgot my aims, and answered my despair with self-pity.

After my time in London, England, I returned to the US in the heyday of the real estate bonanza. When I had initially left for Europe in 2003, I had sold my 1.5 Bedroom Condo in Miami Beach close to the ocean for $140,000.

When I returned in 2006, the same place was worth $300,000.

Unfortunately, the three years in Europe had depleted my funds, and buying or renting a home in my beloved South Beach was out of the question.

My wife Natalia was a flight attendant with US Airways based in Philadelphia. So, we thought to try the Northeast Coast and moved to Philly, the City of Brotherly Love and Sisterly Affection.

But there as well, we could not afford anything. Prices were through the roof, and living in a substandard studio apartment in some dark alley in the city was different from our liking.

Searching for alternatives, I found an advertisement in the paper announcing the revitalization of a part of Camden, NJ, just over the Walt Whitman Bridge close to the Schuylkill River, dividing Philadelphia from Camden.

We went and were blinded by the developer's offer due to the state's funded revitalization effort in Fairview, a charming - so we thought- quiet neighborhood at the first exit in New Jersey off the Walt Whitman Bridge.

We bought a three-story house with a large basement on a large lot with old trees and ample space for gardening. It was $80,000. Low interest, plus a three percent down payment to sweeten the deal. The exact price would have awarded us only a closet in Philadelphia.

. . .

However, we did not realize that Camden was, in those years, the "Murder Capital" of America, the rate of murders happening per capita in US cities.

Walking the adjoining streets to reach a store or restaurant displayed all the dark sites of an impoverished community left to rot without decent jobs, poor education, food deserts, and apparent neglect for the predominantly black inhabitants.

Heroin-addicted prostitutes lined the back alleys; drunken homeless men lay in their excrements; police sirens blasted through the night with fearful neighbors and liquor stores instead of fresh food supermarkets.

Although the two years we lived in Camden were very difficult, I could at least often visit Walt Whitman's house until he died in 1892.

One day on my drive to his house, I was aware of the science fiction scenes of a planet deprived of beauty and decency. Burned-out houses with smashed windows stripped of all human character lined the streets. Abandoned cars were balancing on some bricks with nothing besides the reminiscence of something that drove one time ago. Young people who were supposed to be at school lingered instead at street corners selling everything that gives a high. Open lots filled with trash and debris that was once possessions cherished by former lives.

Visiting Whitman's house on Mickle Street, Camden, always created some awakening shocks. Although in Walt's time, this was downtown Camden, and the house was just part of four surviving homes with nothing left around them. From his entrance to the other side, one can see the big, ugly blocks of the Camden County Main Prison Facility.

How could a city planner imagine a fear-evoking prison building, with all the barbed wire and fences, appearing heartwarming next to the parks and decent housing for its people in downtown Camden?

This shows how life is like a prison for those who sleep and do not realize their sleep. Life is a high-security facility for people who have nothing in their lives and those who have everything in their lives. It makes no difference.

Walt Whitman taught me not to judge and despise the unfortunate but to embrace and love them. We are not different from each other. We have multitudes in us. Our blessing is having received the beautiful gift of reflecting on our meaning in life and realizing that *"Good is in All."*

"Wonderful to depart!

Wonderful to be here!

The heart, to jet the all-alike and innocent blood!

To breathe the air, how delicious!

To speak – to walk – to seize something by the hand!

To prepare for sleep, for bed, to look at my rose-colored flesh!

To be conscious of my body, so satisfied, so large!

To be this incredible God, I am!

To have gone forth among other Gods, these men and women I love."

For Walt Whitman, the world is a miracle, no matter where we are and what we do.

Everything is in the Present for him; nothing else matters. He sees the meaning of the world in the things around him, and he is not afraid to pronounce himself more significant than any institution, government, or theory. He is not scared to see the different sides of himself as well. The opposites, the shortcomings. And with that, he announces his ideology to the world and his fellow man: *"Whoever you are! Claim your own at any hazard."*

He knows that he contradicts himself. He is ok with this understanding that he contains *"multitudes."* He resists anything better than his diversity. He knows he exists *"as I am; that is enough."*

"Leaves of Grass" by Walt Whitman is a rich source for us Seekers. For us who are trying to be in this Moment, for us who understand that we need to accept ourselves and love ourselves, to Be Present, and to love others.

Love is the ultimate difference between us Seekers and the men and women who became Gods. They were ready and destined to awaken because they could love. They loved themselves, other human beings, the world, and everything in it.

We are beginners in this business of love, but even just grasping glimpses of this divine ability to embrace, not to judge but to understand, and to accept, is the only requirement for Awakening. To love is to be Present. To be Present is to love. It is simple yet unimaginable for us who have just lit the candle to see in the dark.

Walt Whitman understands that nobody can be convinced by arguments or reasoning: *"We convince by our presence."* So, he invites us to travel with him on this exciting *"road for traveling souls."* But do not forget to *"take your lovers on the road with you"* because this road is not denial or frugality; this road is about Abundance, Love, and Compassion.

He gives us his hand to travel the road with him but cautions us not to stay sleeping and dallying back there with all our possessions and identifications.

We must start. We cannot wait any longer. Like Walt, we are divine inside and out, and our touch will make us holy and whatever else we touch on this journey.

However,

"Not I, not anyone else can travel that road for you; you must travel it for yourself."

We need to find our individual mentor for this journey into Consciousness, yet our guide will only show us the Way; we must walk it ourselves.

Fortunately, my guide, Walt Whitman, revealed himself to me. Sometimes on my way, though, I did forget him; I refused to listen to his voice, which made me forget his lessons. But he was always there waiting for me when I finally realized that my self-pity, indulgence, and anger had become old and unsuitable. He was there to embrace me again, and now here I am.

This is part of Awakening. When our struggle To Be Here Now is the fiercest, when the evil forces of our enemies have found a foothold through identification or negativity, our conscious light only flickers weakly. These times can last minutes, hours, weeks, and even years. I experienced these desperate timeframes in my Journey To Be for long periods. Yet, I became more robust and focused, having relieved the person I did not want to be, the "evil clown" in all its color and manifestations.

So do not despair. As Wolfgang von Goethe, the famous German Renaissance Man, Writer, and Conscious Being noted:

"Continue Because You Must!"

The "Body Electric," Walt Whitman's expression of the complete human being, praises men and women as the essential task. What will you be if you do not love your neighbor? If you do not love your fellow man and woman in the way you'd want to be loved as well? Do you remember a man or woman you admired, his walk, her sweet quality, the movement of her hair? You see them pass, noticing they might be the most beautiful poem you have ever read. Now you see the folds of her dress, the strong shoulders of the man in front of you, you see yourself in the perfection of others, and you understand that you are Here Now, where you always wanted to be and never dared to arrive.

I know it well, the despair and suffering. But I started praying to remember this moment and to say thank you for the criticism arriving in my thoughts. That is when I see the poison spreading into my life. Criticism brings Rheumatism, and my hands and back hurt so much. I ask to be free of it and know I am the one shackling myself. So why not be free of it? Why not be thankful for this revelation and ask for forgiveness for the endless times I was too identified to see the sun's rays shining upon me?

We all are the offspring of the Gods. Do you believe that Mythology is not fiction but the reality of life? Did you ever think you could overcome the demons in your life, like the ancient heroes who slashed dragons and monsters?

You can do it if you believe you can. It starts with this simple concept of believing in yourself, the beauty of life, and your right to realize it. After that, everything is here for you to experience, suffer, grow, fall, and stand up again.

Being with those you love is enough to lead you there. Being surrounded by beautiful, laughing friends will clear your mind. Remember the touch of your friend after a friendly game of tennis, the joy of seeing him soothe your loss with a nod of his smiling face?

Like Walt Whitman said, *"All things please the soul, but these please the soul well."*

Throw away your books, art, and religion and enter the realm of yourself, the One you are. Be in the challenge of the lifetimes ahead of you, learning and experiencing your Soul's lessons to awaken. Remember, The Art To Be Here Now is not a strange, foreign concept but accessible right now for you in this Moment. Do you know where you are right now? Are you feeling this book, the light, the temperature? Returning to this Moment is power, power over life and death, and the only destination worth longing for.

I have been in the most amazing places, yet I was consumed by despair, self-pity, and anger during those times. I have been to the ugliest and humblest places in this world and have been blessed by the realization of my existence, the understanding of privilege, and the beauty of my life. I see my Soul reflected now and am thankful.

The Power of Now is here. So lay down this book for a few moments, realize the beauty of your life, see yourself with love, enjoy this Moment, and make it memorable and eternal.

"All the while, it is the Present only."

Walt Whitman

Bonus Book

~

The Sequence of Awakening - Ancient Conscious Teachings Revealed
Spiritual Exercises and Confirmation

Because you have taken an essential step towards your Enlightenment by purchasing this book, I'd like to give you a little gift.

The Ancient Technique for Awakening used by Conscious Schools throughout history

The Sequence of Awakening

is the core of my daily practices to Be Present.

It is a powerful method to

Grasping The Moment
Giving Up Identifications
Experiencing My Life in Harmony With Higher Forces

In addition, I have added some exercises I use in different life situations that help me stay present and not lose my precious Self. It is designed for those situations where we are most mechanical, like eating, driving, or using technical devices.

Get it Now!

Offer Your Advice

I am grateful that you read my book.

Would you be so kind and give me Your Advice in form of a review?

My revelations into Presence have guided my writing, and I hope that some of my experiences and understandings found a sounding board in your mind and heart.

Please leave a review for me on Amazon. Someone may find this book at the right time to continue her journey into Being.

Thank you,
Klaus

Glossary

~

*Higher Centers = Your Soul, Higher Self, Third Eye, Divine Presence. Your destination - the place you are destined to Be. The God-like appearance in your life. Understanding your life as the journey To Be.

*Higher Forces = You can call them Gods, Angels, or Celestial influence. They are metaphysical beings above the level of the human world. Call your angel in your own word - the language does not matter - your experience of this Consciousness leads you to your destination.

*Higher Self = The connection to one's Higher Centers. Presence has appeared in a human being. It is a god-like state and the most authentic part of a human being. It is who you really are.

*Identification = Experiencing only an aspect of one's world. All attention is focused on one thing, excluding everything else. It is being fascinated or concerned about a specific item, event, or person. You are entirely focused on something without the ability to see the larger picture. It also includes the tendency to place one's identity in things that are external and outside of yourself. A mental state of sleep, impossible to Be in the Moment.

*Imagination = Daydreaming. A mental state where one is lost in the past or future and has no concept of the present moment. It also includes misconceptions about oneself and one's abilities. A pleasant dreamlike state that keeps people asleep.

*Lower self, ego, false personality = The part in us that opposes our Awakening. The "evil clown" in us denies Awakening or anything higher than itself. It lives through negativity. It blows itself up to appear necessary, taking space. It refuses any concept of consideration, charity, love, and sacrifice. It is vain; it thrives through the power of worldly possession, believing in the body's absolute. The devil inside us whispers in our ears to take the world's riches instead of the riches of heaven.

The lower self is animal intelligence in human form. It is the most mechanical part of a human being. It functions without any consciousness.

Bibliography

≈

Holy Bible, King James Version, Cambridge University Press, Cambridge 1979

Robert Earl Burton, Self Remembering, Globe Press Books, New York, NY 1991

Rodney Collin, The Theory of Conscious Harmony, Watkins, London 1976

Girard Haven, Creating a Soul, Ulysses Books, Oregon House, CA 1999

P.D. Ouspensky, In Search of the Miraculous, Harcourt, Brace and Co. New York, NY 1949

Walt Whitman, Leaves of Grass, The Modern Library, New York, NY 1950

About the Author

Who is Klaus Labuttis?

Experiencing his first Moments of Presence, Klaus felt himself come alive. A connection with something Higher appeared that has guided him through life since that moment. His journey to discover his own Higher Self has led him to travel and live in numerous countries, spending years in India, Central America, and Europe.

Armed with a deeper understanding of suffering as part of Awakening, he realized that his pathway was chosen by the Gods and that his struggles were part of their divine plan.

Continuing through to today, the desire to share his

understanding and the lessons learned, Klaus is now driven to educate other seekers, so his readers can enlighten and inspire themselves with their passion for Awakening.

Klaus lives with his wife Tanya in Northern California.

Contact:

MindfulKlaus@gmail.com

www.klauslabuttis.org

Visit my website to sign up for "Daily Inspirations" and a weekly "Love Letter" reflecting on my conscious experiences and the miracles I am able to witness.

www.ingramcontent.com/pod-product-compliance
Lightning Source LLC
Chambersburg PA
CBHW071137130626
46553CB00004B/1418